HORRIBLE HISTORIES.

TERRY DEARY

ILLUSTRATED BY
MARTIN BROWN

WALES

READ ALL ABOUT THE NASTY BITS!

SCHOLASTIC

TO DAFYDD LLYR JAMES – THE GREATEST LIVING WELSHMAN .. MAYBE. TD

TO MIKE JONES. GRAND SLAM. AND THANKS FOR THE BOOKS. MB

First published in the UK by Scholastic Ltd, 2008
This edition published 2022
Euston House, 24 Eversholt Street, London, NW1 1DB
Scholastic Ltd Ireland offices at: Unit 89E, Lagan Road, Dublin Industrial Estate, Glasnevin, Dublin 11.

A division of Scholastic Limited

SCHOLASTIC and associated logos are trademarks and/or registered trademarks of Scholastic Inc.
Text © Terry Deary, 2008, 2017, 2022
Cover illustrations © Martin Brown, 2008, 2017, 2022
Illustrations © Martin Brown and Geri Ford, 2008, 2017, 2022

The right of Terry Deary, Martin Brown and Geri Ford to be identified as the author and illustrators of this work respectively has been asserted by them in accordance with the Copyright, Designs and Patents Act, 1988.

ISBN 978 0702 31757 6

A CIP catalogue record for this book is available from the British Library.

Printed and bound in the UK by CPI Group (UK) Ltd, Croydon, CR0 4YY
Papers used by Scholastic Children's Books are made from wood grown in sustainable forests.

2 4 6 8 10 9 7 5 3 1

www.scholastic.co.uk

WHAT'S INSIDE?

FREE: SUPPLEMENT FROM THE ABERGAVENNY ADVERTISER see page 82

EXCLUSIVE: READ ALL ABOUT THE CILMERI KILLER see page 101

INTRODUCTION

Imagine living in a country where the trees drip with human blood.

A country where dragons are out to roast you for dinner.

And where lords invite you to dinner so they can massacre you.

A country invaded by Viking sea-raiders from the west. They smash down your churches or set fire to them if you try to hide inside.

And then Norman knights from the east arrive and build castles and churches (and kill a few peasants who get in their way).

It's a country where gangs of murdering robbers attack you as you walk through their forests.

A country where the punishment for stealing cattle is to have your arms cut off and the punishment for a servant who steals from her mistress is to be burned alive.

Where is this hideously horrible place? Transylvania in the reign of Dracula?

No.

Germany in the fairy tales of the Brothers Grimm?

No.

The prize for guessing is £1000[1].

Here are some clues to help you...

CLUE 1. THIS COUNTRY IS A WESTERN PART OF BRITAIN

PLEASE, SIR, CANADA?

CLUE 2. THIS COUNTRY HAS A LEEK AS ITS NATIONAL PLANT.

HUNGARY?

SO AM I

1. If you guessed correctly please send the £1000 to me, Terry Deary, care of the publisher. Thank you.

Yes, the horrible country is…

…Wales[2]!

The GOOD news is the trees no longer drip with blood and the dragons have disappeared … probably killed off by knights in fireproof knickers. The Vikings have stopped raiding and you can steal as many cattle as you like without having your arms cut off.

All those things happened in Wales's horrible history.

So if you want to know all about these dreadful deeds (not to mention killer squirrels) then read on!

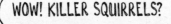

2. You probably cheated and read it on the cover of this book. In that case the prize is doubled to £2000. Please send it as soon as possible because I am a penniless author.

EARLY TIMELINE

The Welsh are the descendants of the ancient Britons. These Celtic tribes ruled most of Britain till the Romans barged in.

Wales hasn't always been horrible. It was quite pleasant in 1306 and again in 1972. But here are some of the horrible highlights...

230,000 BC Neanderthal creatures wander the hills of Wales. They look like humans but act like apes. (Now we call them football supporters.)

AD **43** Roman Emperor Claudius orders an invasion of Britain. The Romans drive the Britons out of England. The only place the Brits can go is west – to Wales. Among them is Caratacus who was from the Catuvellauni tribe, north-west of London. He is defeated in England.

CLAUDIUS: 1
CARATACUS: 0

48 Caratacus stirs up the Silures tribe down in South Wales. He becomes one of the first-ever Welsh heroes. He attacks Roman supplies, and robs and murders tribes (like the Dubonni) who dare to make friends with the Romans.

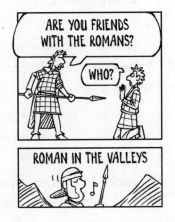

75 The Romans rule Wales.

313 Christianity has started to take over as top religion in Wales. The ancient Welsh priests, the 'Druids', are on the way out … along with their human sacrifices.

CHRISTIANITY RULES, OKAY?

410 The Romans leave. Saxon invaders attack. The Welsh in the south are battered. The ones in the mountains are bothered.

496 Brit hero King Arthur battles the Saxons at Mount Badon. Did Arthur really rule or is he just a story? And was he Welsh? Who knows. This is also the time of saints. Welsh saints set up sites in Wales to teach Christianity.

589 Bishop David dies. He will live on as Saint David ... the patron saint of Wales.

606 The Welsh Christians argue with the Pope. St Augustine is sent from Rome to sort them out. St Gus says:

If the Welsh will not have peace with us, they shall die at the hands of the Saxons.

WE'RE VERY RELIGIOUS

Sure enough, Saxon king Ethelfrith massacres thousands of Welsh at Chester. He kills 1,200 Welsh monks too – just for fun.

784 Offa of Mercia is a powerful Saxon king. He builds Offa's Dyke, marking Wales's eastern border. The Dyke is just a long mound of earth. But Welsh who cross it risk their lives.

CROSS THIS AND IT'S OFF A WITH YOUR HEAD

GET OFF-A THE MOUND!

850 First report of a Viking attack on Wales. They kill King Cyngen. The Welsh need a hero to unite them. And they find one in the great Rhodri Mawr.

878 Rhodri Mawr dies fighting the English. He was the first Welsh ruler to unite the Welsh tribes under one rule. During his reign, the Vikings increase their raids.

927 Welsh kings give in and allow the English to be their king of kings.

1039 The last of the Welsh High Kings, Gruffydd ap Llywelyn, takes the throne. By 1057 he has battled and murdered his way to all the thrones of Wales.

1063 Gruffydd beaten by Harold of England then murdered ... probably by his own men.

HEADS AND TAILS

The ancient Welsh had a thing about heads. A lot of their legends were about heads ... usually dead heads.

HEAD BOY BRAN

In the Welsh legends the greatest Welshman was Bendigeidfran ... or Bran for short. Well, when I say 'short' he was really 'long'. He was so tall he paddled across the Irish Sea to fight the Irish.

Why would he want to attack the Irish?

Because they insulted his sister, Branwen.

Here is her terrible tale…

Once upon a time there was a lovely Welsh princess called Branwen. She was so lovely the Irish King Matholwch wanted to marry her. Beautiful Branwen said, 'Yes … please.' (You should always say 'please'.)

But Branwen's nasty brother was so jealous he attacked the Irish king's horses … nastily. He sliced their lips back to their teeth, and their ears back to their heads, and their tails to their backs – and wherever he could get a grip on their eyelids, he would cut these back to the bone. That was nasty, wasn't it?

Matholwch felt a real fool so he took Branwen back to Ireland and punished her. He made her slave in the kitchens and sent a butcher to slap her around the head every day. Poor princess. So the brave Branwen tamed a starling to sit on the edge of her bread bowl. Let's hope it didn't poop in the pastry! She taught it to talk.

'Starling,' she said, 'fly to Wales and tell my big brothers how unhappy I am.'

'Squawk,' said the starling.

Brother Bendigeidfran walked over from Wales while the rest of the army went in ships. The Welsh massacred every living Irish person except for five Irish women. The Irish killed every Welsh soldier except seven heroes. Even Bran died with a poisoned spear in his foot. As he died he told his brothers, 'Cut off my head and take it home to Britain. Bury it in London and I will protect the country from danger.'

Then the heroes took Branwen home along with Brother Bran's big head.

What a happy ending!

No.

Branwen landed at the Welsh island of Anglesey and looked back at Ireland. She wept, 'Oh, Ireland. Everyone massacred ... Except five women who are expecting babies.' Then she looked at Wales and wept. 'Oh, ohhhh! Britain! All the greatest warriors dead ... Except the seven warriors who brought Bran's head home. Woe to me that I was ever born. Two good islands have been ruined because of me.' Then she looked at her brothers and wept, 'Oh, I think I will die of a broken heart.'

And that's just what she did! They buried her.

Sorry but we don't know what happened to the starling.

The End

Bran's head was buried in London. But someone stole it along with two other skulls from the graveyard and so Britain was never safe again.

The law officers never found out who stole those three skulls.

This may sound like a silly story. But it tells us something about the Celts who lived in Wales in ancient times…

HEADLINES

A ncient Celts believed in the power of the head. Nine of these foul facts are true. Can you spot the one false head-line?

Ancient Celts...

1 ...believed severed heads could speak, tell the future and give you warnings

2 ...said dead heads were extra powerful in groups of three

3 ...stuck rotting heads on poles at the gates of their hill forts

4 ...threw heads into lakes and rivers as a gift to the gods

5 ...nailed enemy heads to their walls as a sort of decoration

6 ...made the brains into a sort of concrete ball to stop them rotting

7 ...invented rugby and played it with human heads

8 ...buried some of their dead with the head removed and placed between the legs

9 ...had a goddess with three heads called Ellen

10 ...kept enemy heads pickled so they could be taken out and looked at by visitors.

HEADS YOU WIN

Lopped heads appear in lots of Welsh tales. At one time heads must have been bouncing round Celtic lands like lottery numbers in a drum. St Llud, St Justinian, St Nectan and St Decuman all lost their heads and springs of fresh water gushed from the ground where they fell.

WELL, WELL, WELL!

One of the most famous loppings was St Gwenfrewi (or Winifride in English) – around AD 600.

• Winifride was a nun. She was also the niece of Saint Beuno, an abbot in sixth-century Wales.

• Young Welsh Prince Caradoc ap Alyn loved her but she refused to marry him.

• This upset the young prince so he drew his sword and cut off her head.

•As her head hit the ground a spring of water gushed out of the dry rock.

• Along came St Beuno, stuck her head back on her body and she was restored to life, with just a thin white line round her neck to show her little accident.

• Beuno was not so kind to Caradoc. The saint cursed the prince till the earth opened up and swallowed him.

Winifride's well waters are now said to cure illnesses and the well in Holywell, North Wales is still visited by tourists.

Get well in
HOLYWELL

6 refills included with every souvenir water bottle

THE CURSE OF NANT GWRTHEYRN!

In ancient times three Holy Men came to Nant Gwrtheyrn to convert it to Christianity. But the head man of the village was a pagan and drove them out with stones and abuse.

The Holy Men cursed the village – no one would be born there, no one would marry there ... And the village itself would die!

Sure enough, no one was born there for hundreds of years and the village began to die. Till, one year, two young people of the village fell in love and decided to marry.

It was then the custom for the bride to go and hide.

Off she went. But search as he might the groom couldn't find his bride. The search went on all day – then the next day… And after a week he gave up.

Which is just what he did.

Years later a storm brought down some old oaks on the cliff top. One oak split open and there, inside, was the skeleton of a woman … with scraps of a wedding dress clinging to the bones!

The bride had hidden herself in the hollow tree and become trapped.

The curse had claimed another unhappy victim.

DREADFUL DRUIDS

When the Romans arrived the Welsh hid in the mountains. The Welsh warriors attacked the Romans quickly … then dashed back to the mountains. Today this is called 'guerrilla' warfare.

Roman governor Ostorius died. It was said he was worn out by the struggle. Before a new governor could arrive, a Roman army was defeated by the Silures tribe in South Wales. It was Rome's greatest defeat in Britain.

Roman writer Tacitus says…

The Silures, a fierce people, were now brave in the might of Caratacus; by many battles he had raised himself far above all the other generals of the Britons.

The Romans set off to attack the rebels on Anglesey. That's where the Welsh war-priests, the druids, were gathered.

The Romans probably marched through Cheshire. And it is just possible that the druids tried to stop them there with powerful magic.

A human sacrifice. Go to the British Museum today (in London) and see the Lindow man…

Of course, Lindow man COULD have just been a cruel execution, not a sacrifice.

The Romans wanted to seek out the druid priests who were stirring up all the trouble. As they marched through the mountains the Welsh ambushed them. The Romans couldn't bring them into a proper battle on flat ground, the way they liked.

At last the Romans reached the Menai Strait (between Wales and the island of Anglesey) and crossed it. The Welsh thought they'd be safe from the Romans. But the Romans rode and swam across. The Roman writer Tacitus described the scene when Suetonius Paulinus invaded. It makes pretty gruesome reading…

> On the far shore stood the forces of the enemy with women dashing through the ranks like the furies; their dress was black, their hair wild, and they carried torches in their hands. The druids stood around the fighting men, screaming horrible curses, with their hands raised towards the heavens. They struck terror into the Roman soldiers; it was as if the Roman limbs were frozen, they could not move.

Tacitus was a Roman. So OF COURSE he made Paulinus sound like a hero!

> The brave Paulinus said they would not be scared by a rabble of women and madmen. The Romans attacked. They smote[3] all the Welsh and wrapped them in the flames the Welsh had lit. The Romans killed everyone who stood in their way, including the women and druids who carried no weapons.

3. 'Smote' is a really good word. It means 'battered' but sounds more exciting. Next time you've a problem in the school yard say, 'please, sir, the school bully smote me mightily!' That'll get him in detention for two years at least.

Paulinus's men overran the island, dragged out victims who tried to hide and tore down the sacred temple where the druids had carried out their sacrifices.

The druids thought it was a holy duty to soak the altars with enemy blood.

Tacitus was shocked. He said…

The trees dripped with human blood. The druids read the future by slicing open humans on their altars and watching which way they fell!

The Romans conquered most of Wales in the end. There were rich gold mines in Wales and that's what the Romans really wanted. The Roman leader Agricola almost wiped out the tribes in Snowdonia … the Hammer Men!

But the Romans didn't try to settle in the 'wild country' – the mountains and the forests in the north.

Tribes were left alone to keep the old ways alive. And poets told tales of a great leader who would arise and lead the Welsh to glory.

SMASHING SAXONS

The British King Vortigern took over when the Romans went home (or went Rome) around AD 410.

Bye-bye, Romans. Good news for Wales? No. Bad news. Very bad news. Because the Saxons moved in to England. Savage Saxons.

In AD 449, Vortigern's best soldiers were massacred by the Saxons. He escaped to Wales[4]. The Saxons brought their slicing swords and awful axes to Wales.

4. Vortigern had invited the enemy Saxons into his castle for a party and the Saxons brought knives. Big sharp knives. They murdered Vortigern's mates. There is a word for people like Vortigern. That's right, the word is spelled 's-t-u-p-i-d'.

The monk Gildas writes…

> *Many were caught in the mountains, and were murdered.*
> *Others, starving, gave themselves up to be slaves for ever.*
> *They ran the risk of being killed on the spot. To be honest*
> *that was the best thing that could happen to them. The ones*
> *who lived were sent away, over the seas, wailing and in*
> *misery.*

I DON'T AGREE WITH WHALING

DEADLY DRAGONS

There is a dragon on the Welsh flag. Why?
In North Wales there is an old hill fort,
known as Dinas Emrys. There is a legend that
Vortigern tried to build his castle here. But every
night, when the work stopped, the tower fell down.

★ COMPETITION TIME! ★

DESIGN A CASTLE
must stay standing

TOP PRIZE:
One night in the castle before you go home

His diary must have looked pretty boring that first week...

1 APRIL AD 450
TODAY THE WELSH STARTED BUILDING ME A CASTLE AT DINAS EMRYS.

2 APRIL AD 450
WOKE UP AND BLOW ME! THE CASTLE HAS FALLEN DOWN IN THE NIGHT. THE LADS STARTED BUILDING IT AGAIN.

3 APRIL AD 450
WOKE UP AND BLOW ME! THE CASTLE HAS FALLEN DOWN IN THE NIGHT. AGAIN. THE LADS STARTED BUILDING IT AGAIN, AGAIN.

4 APRIL AD 450
THE CASTLE HAS FALLEN DOWN IN THE NIGHT. AGAIN, AGAIN. THE BUILDING LADS ARE GETTING A BIT FED UP.

14 APRIL AD 450
BUILDING LADS ON STRIKE. FED UP. SO I SPOKE TO AN OLD WISE MAN.

'SO, WISE OLD MAN,' I SAID, 'WHY DOES MY TOWER KEEP FALLING DOWN?!'

HE SAYS, 'THERE IS AN OLD CUSTOM IN THIS PART OF BRITAIN THAT SAYS A NEW HOUSE MUST HAVE A BLOOD SACRIFICE! SOMETIMES A HUMAN VICTIM IS WALLED UP ALIVE.' NASTY.

HE GOES ON AND SAYS, 'SOMETIMES THEY ARE KILLED AND THEIR BLOOD MIXED WITH THE CEMENT.' MESSY.

'THE BLOOD OF A VICTIM MUST BE SPRINKLED ON THE GROUND,' HE SAID.

'I'LL KILL ONE OF ME WORKMEN!' I SAID – TEACH THE OTHERS NOT TO GO ON STRIKE!

'NO, NO!' THE WISE MAN MOANED, AS WISE MEN DO. 'THE BLOOD MUST BE THE BLOOD OF AN INNOCENT, FATHERLESS BOY!'

SO I TOLD THE BUILDERS, 'RIGHT, LADS! OFF YOU GO AND FIND ME AN INNOCENT, FATHERLESS BOY.'

AT LAST MY MEN BROUGHT BACK A YOUNG BOY NAMED MERLIN.

'RIGHT, LADS, GIVE HIM THE CHOP!'

THEN THIS YOUNG LAD PIPES UP, 'NO! WAIT! DON'T KILL ME! KILLING ME WILL NOT STOP YOUR CASTLE FALLING DOWN.'

'THE WISE MAN SAYS IT WILL,' I SAYS.

'THEN HE'S A STUPID WISE MAN!'

THAT UPSET THE WISE MAN, I CAN TELL YOU. BUT MERLIN WENT ON. 'NO! LISTEN. BENEATH THIS GROUND THERE IS A POOL. AND IN THE POOL THERE ARE TWO DRAGONS – A RED DRAGON AND A WHITE DRAGON. EVERY NIGHT THEY FIGHT AND IT'S THEIR STRUGGLE THAT BRINGS THE TOWER DOWN.'

'AMAZING!' I CRIED. 'WHAT A CLEVER BOY YOU ARE. HERE, LADS, GIVE THE STUPID WISE MAN THE CHOP INSTEAD!'

MERLIN EXPLAINED. 'THE RED DRAGON IS WALES – THE WHITE DRAGON IS SAXON ENGLAND. WHEN THE RED DRAGON DEFEATS THE WHITE THEN PEACE WILL RETURN.'

OH! SO, ALL WE HAVE TO DO IS DEFEAT THE SAXONS. RIGHT, LADS! OFF TO FIGHT THE SAXONS...

Of course Vortigern never did get to defeat the Saxons. That was down to another British leader – the man they knew as Arthur. Merlin joined Arthur and for a while the British defeated the Saxon enemies.

But the legend of the red dragon lives on to this day. (At least the story's short and doesn't 'drag on'. Geddit? Oh, never mind.)

DID YOU KNOW....?

Prince Cadwaladr (633–682) was the first Welsh leader to carry a flag with the Welsh dragon on it. As if it wasn't bad enough having the Saxon attackers to worry about, the Welsh suffered an outbreak of the plague – and this was 500 years before the Black Death. It killed Prince Cadwaladr.

COOL CAULDRON

Before he left, Merlin buried a cauldron full of gold beneath Dinas Emrys. On the mouth of the cave he rolled a huge stone, which he covered up with earth and green turf, so that it was impossible for anyone to find it.

This treasure is meant for some special person. When the special person comes to the Dinas a bell will ring to invite them into the cave. The stone will roll away as soon as their foot touches it.

DID YOU KNOW....?

When Dinas Emrys was dug up in the 1950s they really did find a deep pool. Spooky or what?

TERRIBLE TALE OF SAINT DAVID

The Welsh have their own saint to guard them. David. He died on 1 March 589 so 1 March became St David's Day.

He became a bishop in Wales and then archbishop – top Christian man. But he was a bit of an odd person.

Even his miracles were a bit odd.

Dave's miracles 1

One day Bishop David had to preach at Llanddewi Brefi. But there were crowds of people at Llanddewi waiting to hear the bishops preach – it was a sort of competition and the one who spoke the clearest would become the archbishop.

The other bishops stood on piles of clothes to be heard but they failed. Then along came David. He didn't have to stand on a pile of clothes. He just began to preach and a mountain rose under his feet. It was a miracle!

We know this is true because the mountain is still there at Llanddewi Brefi!

HORRIBLE HISTORIES NOTE

There must be HUNDREDS of mountains
in Wales. Wales is famous for its mountains.
Why did Dave need to make another one?
Why not just stand on one of the
hundreds that are
already there?

> WHAT DID 'E SAY?

> DUNNO. HE'S STANDING ON TOP OF A MOUNTAIN

Dave's miracles 2

The Welsh were about to go into battle with the
Saxons near a leek field. They turned to St David
and asked:

> HOW DO WE KNOW WHO'S IN THIS BATTLE?

> ALL THE WELSH SOLDIERS MUST WEAR A LEEK ON THEIR HATS

And they did. They won the battle and the leek
has been the sign of Wales ever since … along with
the daffodil and the dragon. But it's a bit difficult
to stick a dragon on your hat.

HORRIBLE HISTORIES NOTE

**What was a saint doing killing Saxons? Eh?
Doesn't sound a very Christian thing to me!**

And talking about killing…

Dave's miracles 3

David ran a tough monastery and it is said some
monks didn't like it…

See? What sort of saint is that? Hundreds of dead Saxons in battle not to mention dead dogs and crows. He was just a pet-poisoning priest.

MURDERED MONKS

The Welsh became Christians but, at first, their old enemies the Saxons weren't. The Welsh travelled far and wide spreading the word of God.

But they wouldn't go to England.

The historian Bede (672–735) said the Welsh missionaries refused to preach to the Saxons in England.

You can hear those old monks chanting it, can't you?

So the church of Rome had to send St Augustine over to convert the Saxons.

The trouble was, when Augustine got to Britain he found the Welsh Christians didn't worship the same way as the Roman Christians.

So Augustine said the Welsh Christians should meet him and talk about the problem. They agreed to meet at an oak tree. St Dinas of Bangor Iscoed monastery set off to meet him.

Bangor Monastery had 2,400 monks – they took turns so 100 were singing each hour of the day!

Must have made sleeping a bit difficult!

Anyway, Dinas met Augustine at St Augustine's Oak. But things didn't go to plan.

A wise man told Dinas:

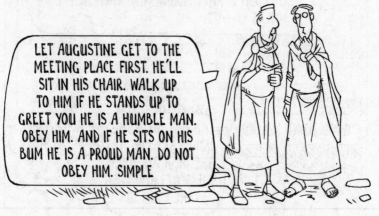

LET AUGUSTINE GET TO THE MEETING PLACE FIRST. HE'LL SIT IN HIS CHAIR. WALK UP TO HIM IF HE STANDS UP TO GREET YOU HE IS A HUMBLE MAN. OBEY HIM. AND IF HE SITS ON HIS BUM HE IS A PROUD MAN. DO NOT OBEY HIM. SIMPLE

Of course Augustine didn't stand up. So the Welsh refused to take his orders.

Augustine said God would destroy Dinas and his monastery.

That Augustine may have been made a saint but he wasn't very saintly. He took no chances. Just in case God didn't take revenge on the Bangor monastery, Augustine made sure the Saxons did.

He went to the Saxon King Ethelfrith and said:

KING ETHELFRITH, WHY NOT ATTACK CHESTER EH? AND THERE IS A MONASTERY AT BANGOR ABOUT TWELVE MILES SOUTH OF CHESTER SO IT MIGHT BE A GOOD IDEA TO ATTACK THAT WHILE YOU'RE THERE[5]

Ethelfrith set off to attack Chester. A messenger went from Chester to beg Ethelfrith for peace.

The messenger was sent back to Chester … in a box … chopped into little pieces.

Ethelfrith attacked Chester then turned on the monastery. In all 1,200 monks were murdered. Only 50 lived to tell the tale.

5. Of course some Christians say Augustine did not have the monks murdered. They reckon he died in AD 605 – ten years before the Battle of Chester in 615.

CRUEL CADWALLON

The Battle of Chester cut the Welsh off from their friends, the Britons in the north of England.

So King Cadwallon of Gwynedd decided to fight the Saxons. He joined up with the pagan King Penda. Cadwallon won a battle near Doncaster, killed King Edwin of Northumbria and lopped off his head…

But he wasn't a very nice man. The historian and monk Bede said…

> At this time there was a great slaughter both
> of the church and of the people of Northumbria.
>   The barbarian Cadwallon was even more cruel
> than the heathen Penda. Cadwallon was a Christian
> by name but a barbarian at heart and spared neither
> women nor children. With beastly cruelty he put all
> to death by torture and for a long time raged through
> all their land, meaning to wipe out the whole of the
> English nation from the land of Britain.

Of course Bede was an English historian. He
WOULD say that.

But Cadwallon only ruled a year before getting
himself killed at a battle near Hexham in 635.

OFFA THE AWFUL

By the 780s the English in the Midlands were fed up with Welsh raids…

I'M FED UP WITH WELSH RAIDS

AND US WELSH ARE FED UP WITH THE ENGLISH RAIDS

So both sides were probably quite pleased when the English King Offa (757–796) came along and built his massive Offa's Dyke – a great wall of earth to mark the boundary.

There were no forts like there were on Hadrian's Wall. Most people thought it was like a fence between two gardens – English to the east side, Welsh to the west.

If a Welshman was found to the west of the dyke he was punished … horribly.

Offa's Toffee Waffles
Perfect with a cuppa!

Offa was a cruel man. We don't know if the Welsh liked the idea of a border or not. It didn't matter…

43

BAD BARDS

The Welsh love poetry and their singing poets – 'bards' – were treated like kings. There is still a great festival every year where bards battle to be crowned the best. It's called the Eisteddfod.

The old Celtic bards were like pop singers today – but without the guitars.

And, like top pop singers, they were well paid.

The bad news is that it was a long hard job to train as a Celtic poet. A pop singer probably trains for 12 whole minutes – a Celtic poet would train for 12 years.

He learned very long poems – 80 in the first six years. He learned another 95 in the next three years and by the end of the 12 years he knew 350 story poems … if he survived, that is.

Because learning a story poem of an hour or so long took a lot of hard thinking.

Next time your SATs are due and you need to learn some facts then try the Welsh way…

1. LIE DOWN ON THE FLOOR OF A ROOM WITH NO WINDOWS

NO BED EITHER JUST A HARD FLOOR

2. PLACE A HEAVY STONE ON YOUR STOMACH

JUST LIKE EATING ONE OF YOUR MOTHER'S SCONES

3. PLACE A BLANKET OVER YOUR HEAD

SPOOKY

4. REPEAT THE POEM 100 TIMES LIKE A PARROT

WHO'S A PRETTY BOY THEN?

5. AFTER 12 YEARS BE TESTED.

MARY HAD A LITTLE… DAMN, I'VE FORGOTTEN IT!

The poet would travel round with a metal model of a tree branch. It would have bells on and they would ring as he rode along or entered a feasting hall.

The branch would tell you what sort of poet he was: a bronze branch for a new poet, a silver branch for an expert and a gold branch for someone who was top of the pops.

He'd swagger around in a cloak covered in birds' feathers – the feathers of white and coloured birds were worn below the belt, the crests and necks of mallard ducks were worn above the belt[6]. Some say a swan's head dangled down his back.

TERRIBLE TALES

Imagine the nastiest thing possible. That's the sort of thing the Celtic poets would sing about.

In the Dark Ages there was a lot to be miserable about.

When the Prince of Powys, Cynddylan, died in 655 the bards wrote the mournful poem, 'The Song of Heledd'[7].

---

6. Don't try making one of these. You'll just look quackers.
7. Heledd means 'salt-pit' you know. Imagine calling a child 'salt-pit'? Why not pepper-pot? Or jar of mustard? What were her parents thinking of? Poor little Salt-pit.

Heledd was the sister of Cynddylan who lost all her brothers in a battle to save a place called Tern.

THE SONG OF HELEDD

My brothers were killed at a single stroke
Defending the poor town of Tern.
The blood on the fields was as common as grass
And the hall of Cynddylan is burned.

Cynddylan would ride into battle and kill.
His heart was as wild as a boar,
The enemy corpses were two layers deep
When my brother he rode out to war.

Cynddylan he rode in a fine purple cloak
And he treated his guests like a lord.
Now his white flesh it lies in a coffin of black.
His life claimed by the vile Saxon hordes.

Cynddylan will never return to his hall.
It is dark, there's no fire and no bed.
I lie sick and feeble, and stroke the dark hair
That will never grow grey on his head.

Cheerful stuff.

BAD FOR BARDS

It was said the English king, Ed the first,
massacred the Welsh bards because they were
chanting Welsh poems.

Years later the poet Mary Hannay Foott wrote a
dreadful poem all about the massacre. Here is a little
bit of the vile verse to show how bad poetry can be…

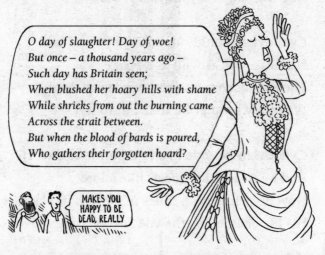

O day of slaughter! Day of woe!
But once – a thousand years ago –
Such day has Britain seen;
When blushed her hoary hills with shame
While shrieks from out the burning came
Across the strait between.
But when the blood of bards is poured,
Who gathers their forgotten hoard?

MAKES YOU
HAPPY TO BE
DEAD, REALLY

HORRIBLE HISTORIES TRUTH

It didn't happen. There was a story that King
Edward I ordered the burning of Welsh books
in London. That got confused with the legend
that the Welsh book-writers were burned.

They weren't! Not even singed. Don't believe
everything you read in a poem.

VICIOUS VIKINGS

The Vikings settled in Dublin around AD 840. From there it was just a quick sail across the Irish Sea to rob the Welsh. Churches were great targets. All those golden crosses and powerless priests.

The Welsh started to build their churches in valleys so the Vikings couldn't see them from the sea.

They also tried praying to God for bad weather to keep the Viking ships away.

There's a story about Bishop Morgeneu who suffered a Viking attack. In the year 999 the Church of St David at Menevia was destroyed and Bishop Morgeneu killed by Vikings.

You can just picture it, can't you? The villagers are having a church service.

There's a tap on the door...

An old woman hurries into the church.

WOE IS ME! THERE'S A VIKING WARSHIP JUST PULLED UP ON THE SHORE. THEY'LL BE HERE ANY MINUTE

The monks gasp. The bishop turns to the people in the church:

MY FRIENDS. THE BLACK NATION ARE AT OUR DOORS AGAIN. THEY'VE LANDED AND WILL SOON BE AT THE DOORS OF THE CHURCH. IF WE GIVE THEM THE LITTLE GOLD AND JEWELS WE HAVE THEY SHOULD GO AWAY. BUT FIRST LET'S TRY LOCKING THE DOOR AND KEEPING QUIET

There is a crash as bolts are rammed shut.

The praying people fall silent. 'Shush! Shush! Shush.'

Suddenly there's a thunderous knock outside the door. Whimpers of fear inside. Singing of Vikings from outside.

The bishop cries out:

GO AWAY, THERE'S NO ONE HERE!

The Viking leader doesn't believe him.

There's a crash and a splintering of wood.

The Viking picks up a cross. 'And I thought you said you had no gold. What is this?'

The Viking decides the common people will all be spared – they'll take them alive and sell them as slaves.

The Viking laughs at his own joke.
Then Morgeneu is chopped.
The villagers are taken away and sold as slaves.
No one lives happy ever after. Except for the Vikings.

QUICK QUESTION

Who got the blame for this attack on St David's in 999?
a) Bishop Morgeneu
b) The Vikings
c) The carpenters who made weak doors

---

8 All villains cry, 'Ha! Ha!' I wasn't there in the church myself, but I am sure that's exactly what the Viking leader would have cried. 'Ha! Ha!'… or maybe, 'Heh! Heh!'

DID YOU KNOW...?

The Vikings didn't always win. At the Sunday Battle of Anglesey in 876 the Vikings were beaten. The Welsh reckoned it served them right for going to war on the holy day, Sunday!

NOT AN ARROW ESCAPE

King Magnus Barefoot (1073–1103) was a Viking King of Norway and the Isle of Man.

He attacked North Wales and killed Earl Hugh the Proud in a horrible historical way. A Viking poet told the tale…

It was a long hard battle, fought first with bows, then hand-to-hand. For a long time no one could tell who would win. King Magnus was using a handbow and there was another archer with him, from Halogaland.

Hugh the Proud was putting up a brave fight, and was so well armoured that only his eyes were exposed, so King Magnus suggested to the archer that they should both shoot at Hugh together, and that is what they did.

One arrow struck Hugh's noseguard, but the other entered the eyehole and pierced his head, and there Hugh the Proud fell. King Magnus said it was his arrow that did it.

The Welsh lost a great many troops and in the end they had to run. King Magnus had won a famous victory.

LOVELY LAWS

In the year 927 the Welsh princes said they'd let themselves be ruled by the English king.

But there were still some great Welsh princes.

There were people like Hywel the Good (880–950). (Hywel Dda, the Welsh called him.)

Of course he wasn't all THAT good – he had his brother-in-law killed.

But Hywel did create the 'Law of Hywel', a set of laws that would be in force in Wales for hundreds of years.

HE ASKED FOR IT

They say he took the laws to Rome and had them blessed by the Pope.

They were sensible laws with a bit of respect for women and children. Less of the old 'punishment' and more 'pay cash for your crime'.

56

Hywel's laws saw women as almost equal to men. Almost – but not quite…

In those days women were NOT quite equal to men. A woman slave was worth LESS than a man slave.

DID YOU KNOW...?

Hywel was the first person to get all the bards of Wales together for a contest. It was his idea that was copied in 1880 when the National Eisteddfod group was formed.

The Eisteddfods have been held every year since (except the war years 1914 and 1940).

WILD WEST WELSH

Even with Hywel's laws the Welsh were known to be a bit lawless – especially in the wild West. Between 950 and 1150 a Chronicle of the Princes lists 28 royal murders. But four men had worse fates than being murdered.

A report from the times said...

> PRINCE MEREDITH ATTACKED ANGLESEY, SLAUGHTERED 2000 MEN, CAPTURED HIS OWN BROTHER, AND HAD HIS EYES PUT OUT

Maybe he was hot and wanted to make eyes-cream?

The monk, Gerald of Wales (1146–1223), called the Welsh some nasty things. But remember ... he was being spiteful to the Welsh because of something that happened to him in his monastery. He had been collecting books since his childhood and had one of the best collections of books in Wales. He left them in Strata Florida monastery for the monks to look after while he went to Rome. Where are they now?

So maybe Gerald was getting his revenge when he wrote this…

> *The Welsh people are more keen to own land than any others I know. To steal land they are ready to dig up ditches, to move stones showing the edges of fields and to cross boundaries.*
>
> *They all seem to suffer this lust for land. They are ready to swear that the land has always belonged to their family. There are endless quarrels and murders and burnings; in many cases brother murders brother.*

Gerald lived 200 years after Hywel.

GRUESOME GRUFFYDD

In 1039 Wales was ruled by the last of its High Kings, Gruffydd ap Llywelyn (1000–1063). By 1057 he had battled and murdered his way to all the thrones of Wales.

When he was told he was cruel he replied...

Don't talk to me about killing. I only blunt the horns of the little Welsh lambs in case they hurt their parent!

Gruffydd was especially worried about strong young men – he was afraid they'd grow to challenge him so he had them killed or carved up a bit.

Look at the case of Gruffydd's own nephew, Luarc. He fled for his life and Gruffydd caught up with him...

Dear diary,

Big day today. I mean b-i-g day!

My master Luarc had a visit from his dear uncle, Gruffydd ap Llywelyn. Such a nice man! King Gruff was SO pleased to see Master Luarc! 'Luarc! My dearest nephew!' he cried and hugged my master. 'Here you are! Hiding in this little fortress and guarded by fifty men. I simply don't understand why you'd want to run away from me!'

Luarc was very polite. 'I have to be honest, Uncle – I'm a little worried you may have me murdered.'

King Gruff laughed at that. 'Me! How could you think that of me, my boy? Why, I am the one who protects you! I'm hurt, Luarc, hurt that you could think so badly of me.'

You could see he was hurt by the way he was grinning – trying to hide the pain.

Luarc said, 'It can't be helped, Uncle.'

'Come home with me now,' Gruff said. 'Tell you

what... You can name anyone you want as a hostage for your own safety! Go on! Anyone!'

Luarc thought about this. 'Then I name Hywel.'

King Gruff sighed. 'He's dead.'

Luarc nodded. 'Yes. You arranged for him to be smothered in secret when he was performing a task for you.'

King Gruff shrugged. 'A sad mistake. Name someone else!'

'I name Rotheric.'

'He's dead too,' King Gruff moaned.

'Yes because you met him and embraced him with your right hand as you slew him with a knife in your left hand,' Luarc reminded his uncle.

King Gruff shook his head. 'The knife slipped. Name someone else!'

'I name Theodosius.'

Well, dear diary, you can guess what happened next. Yes, King Gruff said, 'He's dead too.'

And Luarc said, 'He is. Because as he walked and talked with you, you tripped him up with your foot and threw him down a cliff to die on the rocks below.'

'An accident. Name someone else.'

'I name your nephew Meilin...'

'But he's...' King Gruff began.

'...dead too,' Luarc said sternly. 'Not surprising

as you tricked him into one of your strongholds and left him to die loaded with chains in a dungeon.'

Gruff threw his hands up in despair. 'The jailer lost the key! Come home with me, Luarc.'

Luarc shook his head. 'I have a better idea, Uncle. I'll stay here and stay alive. Goodbye.'

Then my master turned to me and said, 'Show him the door, Rhys!'

'It's that wooden thing that fills in the hole in the wall,' I said.

Luarc shook his head. 'No, Rhys. Show my uncle TO the door.'

I led the good king to the door. He muttered to me, 'What a nasty suspicious mind that boy has.'

I had to agree. As I was about to close the door he muttered, 'I don't suppose you fancy putting this poison in his food, do you?'

How I laughed. Such a funny man, King Gruff. Always having a joke – even when so many of his family have had terrible accidents, King Gruff is still joking.

Good night, dear diary.

Clever Luarc lived ... but gruesome Gruffydd ap Llywelyn didn't.

DEADLY DREAM

Gruffydd ap Llywelyn was a jealous man. He was married to Ealdgyth (1034–1086).

He once heard that a young man dreamed about cuddling Ealdgyth and he wanted the young man tortured to death.

His friends said he should take the young man to court instead.

The judge said...

NOW YOUNG MAN, IF YOU HAD CUDDLED THE WIFE OF GRUFFYDD I WOULD HAVE ORDERED YOU TO PAY HIM 1,000 CATTLE

BUT I DIDN'T

YOU JUST DREAMT THAT YOU CUDDLED HER SO I HEREBY SENTENCE YOU TO PAY GRUFFYDD THE 'DREAM' OF 1,000 CATTLE

HOW DO I DO THAT?

YOU MUST TAKE 1,000 CATTLE TO THE SHORES OF A LAKE IN BRECONSHIRE, WHERE KING GRUFFYDD CAN SEE THEM FROM THE OTHER SIDE AND SEE THEIR REFLECTION. THE KING WILL THEN OWN THE DREAM OF THE CATTLE

King Gruffydd was furious ... but for once he didn't get bloody revenge.

DEAD-END GRUFFYDD

In spite of his little faults, Gruffydd ap Llywelyn was a hero. Wales was one country when he was king. For just seven years.

But King Gruff decided to take on the English. Big mistake. The English were led by the great warrior Harold Godwinson.

Harold drove Gruffydd back to Snowdonia and the Welsh king was killed there.

No one is sure exactly HOW great Gryff died. Here is one tale of his end; the tale of an old murder that came back to haunt him.

A man knocked on the door of Gruffydd's hideout:

'I am Cynan ap Iago and I've come to see the great Gruffydd ap Llywelyn. Greetings, Your Highness.'

Gruffydd said, 'Don't I know you from somewhere?'

Cynan replied, 'I'm surprised you remember. It was 24 years ago in Gwynedd.'

'That's when I took over from Iago ap Idwal!' Gruff grinned.

'And how did you take over?' asked crafty Cynan. 'He was murdered. By you, Gruffydd ap Llywelyn.'

Gruffydd tried to deny it. 'I was nowhere near Gwynedd when Iago died.'

That's when Cynan explained the real reason for his visit. 'No, you paid his men to kill him. But you are guilty. You killed my father.'

That's when he drew his sword and killed King Gruff.

Gruff's wife Ealdgyth wasn't too unhappy. She wondered why Cynan was sawing away at Gruff's head. 'I'm taking this head to Harold Godwinson. Proof that I killed his enemy,' Cynan said.

And Ealdgyth said, 'Here! I'm coming with you!'

Three years later Harold was crowned King Harold of England and he married her! She was queen of Wales one year, queen of England the next. But of course Harold died in 1066.

Gruffydd died in 1063. A bad time for Wales to lose her most powerful leader. They had trouble with the Vikings, they had trouble with the English!

But they were going to have more trouble with the next bunch of bullies that were on their way.

The Normans…

MIDDLE AGES TIMELINE

1066 William the Conqueror's Normans arrive in England and head for Wales. Of course some Welsh leaders keep their jobs. People like Rhys ap Tewdwr in Deheubarth (mid-Wales). He makes a deal with William the Conqueror.

1088 But not all the Welsh like the Normans. Rebels throw Rhys out in 1088. He goes to Ireland and gets the vicious Vikings to fight for him. He promises the Vikings that their payment will be all the Welsh men and women they can capture as slaves!

1205 Llywelyn the Great marries Joan. Her dad is King John of England so Llywelyn becomes top man in Wales.

1267 Henry III of England makes Llywelyn ap Gryffudd the 'Prince of Wales'. (He's Llywelyn the Great's grandson.) Henry only does this to stop Llywelyn attacking England.

ROYAL COMPROMISE

1272 Edward I becomes king and sets about turning England into 'Britain'. He ignores Henry III's peace, hates Llywelyn and batters the Welsh. He even has Llywelyn's bride Eleanor kidnapped on the way to the wedding[9].

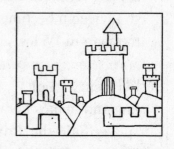

1282 Llywelyn gets into a scrap and dies. England rules Wales and Ed builds massive castles to make sure it stays that way. Llywelyn is remembered as 'Llywelyn the Last Leader'.

1301 Edward I has his own son made 'Prince of Wales' to stop any Welsh lord ever ruling in Wales again.

9. Don't worry ... Llywelyn and Eleanor got together in the end and lived happy ever after and all that. Sort of. She died giving birth to their only baby so Eleanor wasn't too happy after that.

1326 Hugh Despenser is Lord of Glamorgan and Edward II of England is his mate. But when Edward II dies Hugh is arrested at Llantrisant. He is hanged from a massive gallows that is over 15 metres high.

WE HAVEN'T THOUGHT THIS THROUGH, HAVE WE?

1400 Prophets in Wales say that the world is coming to an end in the year 1400. Peasants want to make the most of the time they have left; they booze … and fight. They elect Owain Glyndwr as their leader.

I HAVE BEEN CHOSEN BY GOD TO RELEASE THE WELSH FROM THE SLAVERY OF OUR ENGLISH ENEMIES

YOU'D BETTER BE QUICK, IT'S THE END OF THE WORLD

1415 Glyndwr is beaten by Henry V and disappears – Wales is left in a right mess.

CAN ANYONE FIND OWAIN?

1455 English lords batter each other in the 'Wars of the Roses' – the Lancaster family against the York family. The Welsh fight (and die) for whoever pays them the most. Welshman Thomas Vaughan fights for both sides until in 1469 he is beheaded after the Battle of Banbury. He stops switching sides and stops fighting.

1485 The Battle of Bosworth – last big battle of the Wars of the Roses. King Richard III loses to Henry Tudor fighting under the Welsh dragon flag. It's a Welsh family, the Tudors, who will take over England and Wales for the next hundred years or so. Terrible Tudors. Sadly the family does nothing to help Wales.

1536 Henry VIII makes Wales part of England with the 'Act of Union'. The main language in Wales is now English. Thanks for nothing, Horrible Hen. He also closes all the monasteries.

1593 Hen's daughter Elizabeth I on throne. Puritan John Penry of Breconshire hates the idea of bishops. He is hanged … but many more Welsh will have a thing against bishops. Just wait 150 years and see!

MURDEROUS MIDDLE AGES

You would NOT have wanted to live in Wales after 1066.

• That's right. Those Nasty Normans came along and carved up the country. The Norman earls of Shrewsbury grabbed Pembrokeshire.
• The earls of Hereford took Monmouthshire.
• And the earls of Chester took over the north.
• They called the first earl of Chester Hugh the Fat. He may have been fat but he'd bitten off more than he could chew when he tried to digest the Welsh.

The Welsh were revolting.

ROBBED ROB OF RHUDDLAN

In the 1080s the Vikings were still around to bring wails to Wales.

Some Welsh lords like Gruffydd ap Cynan used Vikings to attack Norman lords. One of the victims was the Norman Robert of Rhuddlan.

One morning in 1088 a knight brought news to Robert's castle at Deganwy. He said, 'Three ships full of Vikings have landed at Orme Head! They are not only stealing the cattle, they are capturing women and children as slaves.'

Robert saw his villages burning and decided to take action.

'Will you ride out to raise your armed men?' the knight asked.

'Don't be ridiculous,' Robert told him. 'The Vikings will be back in Dublin long before I can do that. Let's attack now!'

The knight was shocked. He was wetting himself. 'Just the two of us? Against three boatloads of savage Vikings?'

'One Norman is worth a hundred Vikings,' Robert laughed. 'Let's go!'

What a hero! What an idiot!

Of course when Lord Robert and the knight came face to face with the Vikings they were captured.

QUICK QUESTION

What did the Vikings do with Lord Robert's head?
a) gave it a hero's burial because they admired his courage
b) sent it home to his wife with a letter saying 'Sorry'
c) stuck it on the front of their ship.

Answer: c) It would make the Normans think twice about being heroes in future!

WILD WELSH WOMEN 1 – NAUGHTY NEST

William the Conqueror died in 1087. If the Welsh thought his son, William Rufus, would be any better they would be disappointed.

William Rufus didn't stick to the deals his dad had done. People like Rhys ap Tewdwr (997–1093) were defeated – and he had his head lopped off.

Rhys ap Tewdwr's head was still rolling on the ground when his daughter, Nest, married a Norman lord, Gerald !

But she seemed to like a handsome Welshman better than her Norman husband.

She lived at Cilgerran Castle with her husband, Gerald, but the bold adventurer Owain ap Cadwgan heard of her beauty and went to visit her. He was so in love he decided to take her away.

Owain planned to come back at night with a small band of his best warriors to take the castle and kill Gerald.

They climbed the walls and entered the castle while the guards slept. Then they set fire to some buildings inside the walls and Gerald woke up.

He panicked. Didn't know what to do! So Nest said…

DON'T GO OUT, MY LOVE, FOLLOW ME!

And she led him to a little room … it was the toilet actually.

Toilets in those days were holes in the walls that you sat on and let everything fall into the ditch outside.

Anyway, Nest stuffed her husband down the toilet hole and he escaped.

Nest went off with Owain quite happily.

Of course the king of England made Owain an outlaw and he had to flee. Eight years later he was murdered.

Nest just kept on taking lovers.

She had seventeen children and ended up as the girlfriend of King Henry I of England.

IFOR BACH, BACK FOR HIS LAND

Some Welsh lords decided to fight back against the Normans in crafty ways.

Ifor Bach had his land at Senghennydd taken from him by the Norman earl William of Gloucester.

Earl William moved into Cardiff Castle with his wife and children. They were guarded by 120 Norman soldiers.

In 1158 Ifor decided to get his land back.

Ifor went for a plan that was simple as A, B and C…

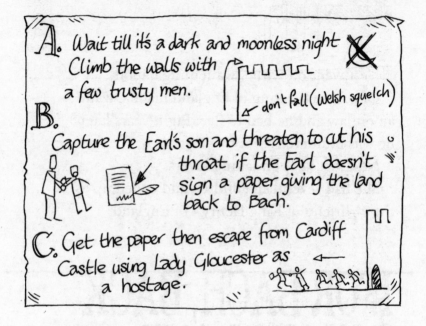

A. Wait till it's a dark and moonless night ✗
Climb the walls with
a few trusty men.
↲ don't fall (Welsh squelch)

B. Capture the Earl's son and threaten to cut his throat if the Earl doesn't sign a paper giving the land back to Bach.

C. Get the paper then escape from Cardiff Castle using Lady Gloucester as a hostage.

It worked.

This story of Welsh daring was very popular with the bards. They wrote lots of poems about it … in Welsh. Children have been reciting them for hundreds of years in schools and festivals.

But you won't understand them, so here's one I wrote in English for you…

William of Gloucester slept in his hall,
Ifor Bach he climbed up his wall.
All the Earl's horses and all the Earl's men.
Couldn't stop Ifor getting his land back again.

Not bard, is it?

AWFUL AT ABERGAVENNY

In 1175 one of the nastiest Norman deeds was done at Abergavenny Castle. The Norman lord, William de Braose, was having a feast.

A Christmas feast! How jolly.

He invited the Welsh chieftain of Gwent, Seisyll. How kind. Especially as it was Seisyll who had murdered William de Braose's Uncle Henry.

William had a very special Christmas present for Seisyll. If there had been newspapers in those days then it would have made the front page.

Abergavenny Advertiser

FREE! ILLUMINATED MANUSCRIPT WITH THE *Advertiser* on Sunday

SILENT KNIGHTS!

'Tis the season to be jolly or … in the case of William de Braose … jolly vicious.

Our Norman lord sent out invitations to his old Welsh enemy, Seisyll the chieftain of Gwent.

'Bring your son and his son Gruffydd, and your top knights,' wily William wrote. 'We'll have a great knight out!' he joked.

The Welsh arrived and took off their weapons – those wonderful Welsh, it's good manners to do that. And then they started drinking and eating. A servant at Abergavenny Castle said this morning,

'There was more drinking than eating. Well, to tell the truth it was the Welsh doing all the drinking – William and the Normans just sipped a little watered wine.'

As midnight struck so did the Normans[10]! First Lord William told his guests, 'I have made a new law that says no Welsh man will ever be allowed to carry a weapon in my lands again.'

Seisyll cried, 'You can never make us obey that, de Braose!' and that's just what the nifty Norman was waiting to hear.

'You've refused to obey an

---

10. Oh, all right, clocks hadn't been invented in those days. Midnight didn't 'strike'. They probably used candles to mark off the hours. If you really want to be fussy let's say, 'As midnight dripped its wax …'

order from the king,' William roared. 'That's treason. The punishment is death. Normans! Kill, them!'

That's when the Normans drew their weapons and hacked Seisyll and his knights to pieces. The only Christmas boxes they'll be getting are wooden boxes to bury them in!

But William's revenge was not complete. William chased Seisyll's wife Gwladus as she tried to escape.

She tried to shield her seven-year-old son in her arms. He was hacked to death.

'Blood all over the rushes on the floor,' our servant said. 'Blood and body bits. We'll have to throw out all the rushes and bury the bodies. We was hoping for a holiday. Some Christmas this has turned out to be!'

William de Braose became known as the 'Ogre of Abergavenny'.

WILD WELSH WOMEN 2 – MATILDA OF HAY

Maud de St Valery was also known as Matilda of Hay ... and Moll Walbee ... just to confuse *Horrible Histories* readers.

She was married to William the 'Ogre of Abergavenny'.

Matilda was a pretty wild warrior in her own way. The Welsh attacked her at Pain's Castle near Hay-on-Wye and she defended it while her husband was away. (The place is still called 'Matilda's Castle'.) In her spare time she had 16 children.

The local Welsh people thought Matilda had powers of witchcraft.

SHE WAS A WITCH! SHE BUILT HAY CASTLE SINGLE-HANDED IN ONE NIGHT CARRYING THE STONES IN HER APRON

WHEN ONE STONE FELL OUT AND STUCK IN HER SLIPPER, SHE PICKED IT OUT AND AND FLUNG IT TO LAND IN ST MEILIG'S CHURCHYARD, THREE MILES AWAY ACROSS THE RIVER WYE

IT MUST BE TRUE. THE NINE-FOOT STONE CAN STILL BE SEEN INSIDE THE CHURCH AT LLOWES

But Mad Matilda tried acting too tough with King John in England.

In 1208 King John told her to send her son William as a hostage – that would make sure she behaved herself. Matilda (madly) refused AND she called John a murderer.

John knew that Matilda must have been in Seine to write that! He had her arrested with her son, William. Matilda's husband was also called William (William de Braose) and, had been Prince Arthur's jailer at the time the prince 'disappeared' in 1202.

So she could have been RIGHT when she said John nobbled his nephew!

King John had Matilda and son William walled up alive in a cell at Windsor Castle with just a piece of raw bacon and a sheaf of wheat.

They were both found dead after 11 days.

After Matilda's cruel death her husband was stripped of all his lands, ran off to France and died the next year.

POWER TO THE PRINCES 1: LOTS OF LLYWELYNS

From about 1200 to about 1300 it was the time of the powerful princes in Wales. Let's start with the first of the Llywelyns, Llywelyn the Great (around 1173–1240).

A history of the time said…

He ruled his enemies with sword and spear. He gave peace to the monks. He enlarged his boundaries by his wars. He gave good justice to all, he made men loyal through fear or love.

First he beat his uncles then he made a deal with King John of England. Llywelyn ruthlessly took control.

LLYWELYN THE FIGHTER

Llywelyn married John's daughter, Joan, in 1205 but that didn't stop him going to war with her dad John in 1211. At first King John suffered. A chronicle said…

And the king came as far as Chester and to the castle of Deganwy. And there his army suffered lack of food to such an extent that an egg was sold for a penny-halfpenny; and they found the flesh of their horses as good as the best dishes.

Neigh, you could say the horses suffered more than King John. But he was mighty miffed.

So John came back with an even bigger army in a few months. A bit of a disaster for the Welsh at first.

And that's when King John showed his nasty streak…

Of course Llywelyn and the Welsh had their revenge for the massacre of the boy hostages.

ROTTEN REVENGE

Around 1200 Gerald of Wales wrote that the Welsh were wonderful warriors … but had some odd habits.

> In war the Welsh are very ferocious when battle begins. They shout, glare fiercely at the enemy, and fill the air with fearsome clamour.
>
> In the first attack they are more than men, and the shower of javelins which they hurl, they seem most terrifying opponents. But, if the enemy fights back, they are driven back. If the enemy fights on the Welsh turn their backs, and run away.
>
> Even though they may be beaten today, and shamefully put to flight with much slaughter, tomorrow they march out again, not the least bit upset by their defeat or their losses. They may not be great in open battle, but they kill their enemy by ambushes and night-attacks.

SAME TIME TOMORROW LADS?

If that makes them sound a bit sneaky, he finished by saying…

In a single battle they are easily beaten, BUT they are difficult to conquer in a long war, for they are not troubled by hunger or cold, and fighting does not seem to tire them.

Their rebellion was the last straw to the English Barons. They turned against John and made him sign a deal called 'Magna Carta'.

It gave power back to Llywelyn in Gwynedd. And it made John give back the land he had stolen.

If we have taken any Welshman's lands, liberties, or anything else without the lawful judgement, these are at once to be returned to them.

Then John died a year later. He died of dysentery – brought on by eating too many peaches.

LLYWELYN THE LOVER

By the year 1230 Llywelyn the Great of Wales had been married to Joan of England for 25 years.

The queen was miserable in Wales but at least she had her son, Dafydd. Until 1230…

Isabel's dad, William de Braose, did a daft thing. He fell in love with Dafydd's mum, Joan. Llywelyn said that William de Braose had given his wife a cuddle! Shocking!

Was it true? Who cares? All we know is they were both locked away at Crokein Manor. Then Llywelyn gave the order…

The guards objected…

So William de Braose was taken away and hanged from a tree. It was the de Braose family that had murdered the Welsh leaders back in 1175 at Abergavenny. They were violent times.

And it wasn't just Llywelyn who was pleased to see de Braose hanged.

Joan thrown off the throne

A report was sent to the king. It said:

> *At that manor which is called Crokein,*
> *de Braose was made to croak.*

Crokein … croak, geddit? And you thought
Horrible Histories jokes were bad?

The report went on:

> *He was hanged from a certain tree and not secretly*
> *or by night but openly and in broad daylight in front of*
> *eight hundred people and more, called together to view*
> *this pitiable and woeful spectacle, and especially those*
> *who hated William de Braose and his sons.*

Did the marriage between the children go ahead?
Of course.

DO YOU ISABEL DE BRAOSE, TAKE DAFYDD TO BE YOUR LAWFUL WEDDED HUSBAND … EVEN THOUGH HE HANGED YOUR DAD?

I DO

DID YOU KNOW...?

They didn't all die by hanging. William de Braose
left a widow, his second wife Eva. She had a
pet squirrel that she adored. One day in 1246
the squirrel scampered over the castle wall.
Eva tried to recover it...

She fell to her death.

TERRIBLE TOWER

Wales had powerful princes in the Middle
Ages. The problem was the chaos they
left when they died.

When Llywelyn the Great died in 1240 his
son Dafydd took over Gwynedd ... no problem.

But Dafydd's brother, Gruffydd, was taken to the Tower of London by English King Henry III in case he caused trouble.

Gruffydd spent most of his life in prisons.

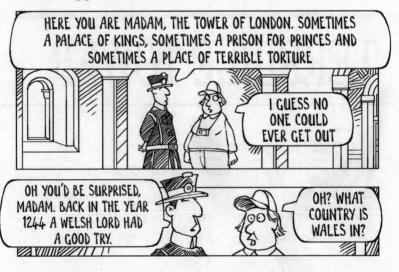

IT'S ROUGH BEING GRUFF[11]

• He had been locked up by King John from 1211 till 1215.
• He was locked up by his own father in 1228 for six years.
• Then he was imprisoned by his own brother at Criccieth in 1239…
• …and handed over to King Henry to be locked in the Tower of London. Mind you, the Tower wasn't that bad. He had his wife for company. And he was put in the comfortable Great Keep there. What happened next…?

HERE YOU ARE MADAM, THE TOWER OF LONDON. SOMETIMES A PALACE OF KINGS, SOMETIMES A PRISON FOR PRINCES AND SOMETIMES A PLACE OF TERRIBLE TORTURE

I GUESS NO ONE COULD EVER GET OUT

OH YOU'D BE SURPRISED, MADAM. BACK IN THE YEAR 1244 A WELSH LORD HAD A GOOD TRY.

OH? WHAT COUNTRY IS WALES IN?

11. Ok, I know it's pronounced Griff, but the joke wouldn't work…

HIS NAME WAS GRUFFYDD AND HE WAS HELD IN THESE ROOMS. NOT EXACTLY A CELL AND HE LIVED QUITE COMFORTABLY. HE WAS A GALLANT WARRIOR

SO HOW COME HE GOT CAPTURED? JOHN WAYNE WOULD NEVER LET THAT HAPPEN

GRUFFYDD WENT TO A PEACE CONFERENCE WITH HIS BROTHER DAFYDD — DAFYDD ARRESTED HIM AND LOCKED HIM UP. HE THEN HANDED GRUFFYDD OVER TO THE ENGLISH KING

THE RAT. WHO CAN YOU TRUST IF YOU CAN'T TRUST YOUR OWN FAMILY?

WHAT DID THIS GUY GRUFFYDD DO? WAIT FOR THE GUARD TO BRING HIS FOOD AND SMASH HIM OVER THE HEAD WITH A FILE HIS FRIENDS HAD CONCEALED IN A CAKE? THAT'S WHAT JOHN WAYNE WOULD'VE DONE

GRUFFYDD MADE A ROPE OUT OF HIS BEDCLOTHES AND CURTAINS. HE TIED IT TO THE END OF HIS BED AND THEN CLIMBED OUT OF THE WINDOW

IT'S TOO NARROW YOU CUTE MAN

NOT EVERYONE IS AS LARGE AS SOME OF OUR VISITORS. GRUFFYDD WAS A HEAVY MAN — BUT NOT FAT. JUST TAKE MY WORD FOR IT, HE SLIPPED OUT THROUGH THE WINDOW

IT'S A MIGHTY LONG WAY DOWN!

HE WAS A BRAVE MAN AND A DESPERATE ONE. HE TOOK THE ROPE OF BEDCLOTHES AND THREW IT OUT OF THE WINDOW

97

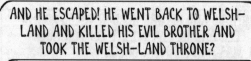

AND HE ESCAPED! HE WENT BACK TO WELSH-LAND AND KILLED HIS EVIL BROTHER AND TOOK THE WELSH-LAND THRONE?

NOT EXACTLY MADAM ... THE BOY SCOUTS HADN'T BEEN INVENTED BACK IN 1244. HIS KNOTS WERE USELESS. THE ROPE PARTED AND HE FELL. BROKE HIS NECK

OH MY WHAT A WONDERFUL STORY! WAIT TILL I TELL THE FOLKS BACK IN WICHITA! YOU MUST LET ME GIVE YOU A TIP. HERE'S ONE OF THOSE CUTE 20-PENCE PIECES AND IT'S ALL RIGHT, YOU DON'T HAVE TO GIVE ME ANY CHANGE

WHY, THANK YOU, MADAM

SLAM!

HEY! EXCUSE ME! HOW DO I GET OUT?

YOU DON'T MADAM. NO ONE EVER ESCAPES FROM THE TOWER NOT EVEN A WELSH PRINCE

DAFYDD DIED IN 1246 – TWO YEARS AFTER HIS BROTHER, GRUFFYDD

SERVES HIM RIGHT, BETRAYING HIS BROTHER LIKE THAT

GRUF DIED 1244

DAF DIED 1246

Gruffydd's four sons divided Wales between them – and then started fighting one another.

Llywelyn ap Gruffydd came out top dog.

LLYWELYN THE LAST

Llywelyn ap Gruffydd (1223–1282) was also known as Llywelyn ap Gwynedd and Llywelyn the Last.

Of course he didn't KNOW he was going to be the last. He probably thought he'd be the first of a long line of Welsh princes.

English King Henry III already had enough problems – in fact even his friends could be stroppy. Friends like Walter de Clifford…

MESSENGER MUNCH

At Llandovery Castle the Norman lord was Walter de Clifford. One day Henry III sent a messenger to Walter…

Dear Walter
Just a little invite for you to pop over to London to see me. Nice party Tuesday week – be there 7.30pm for 8pm start
By order of your monarch
Henry (the third)

Walter was furious. 'This is an order to attend his court. It is a demand. No English king tells ME what to do!'

JOB VACANCY

The Norman's doorman is no more, man!
Must be good at delivering bad news

Then he grabbed the messenger and said…

Walter made him eat every scrap.

And that was a FRIEND of Henry III.

But with so many problems Henry III couldn't punish him. No wonder he gave Llywelyn the title 'Prince of Wales'.

Henry III died and along came King Edward I of England. Seriously bad news for Llywelyn and Wales…

CILMERI KILLER

Llywelyn, now Prince of Wales, had to fight to keep Wales for the Welsh. In 1282 he rebelled against King Edward of England.

He burned Edward's castles and fought Edward's troops. Edward was furious. But while Llywelyn was away gathering a new army, the English attacked first.

The Welsh were beaten near Builth Wells. They say 3,000 Welsh surrendered, and put down their weapons – then the English slaughtered them[12].

Llywelyn heard the battle and rushed back. But it was a trap. He'd been betrayed.

The story says…

WHEN LLYWELYN GOT TO THIS BRIDGE HE MET AN ENGLISH KNIGHT, STEPHAN DE FRANKTON, WHO CHALLENGED HIM TO A FIGHT

Llywelyn was the most wanted man in Britain – but this Stephen de Frankton had no idea he was fighting the Prince of Wales.

Llywelyn wasn't wearing any armour – just a tunic. Stephen de Frankton charged at him with a lance…

The knight ran Llywelyn through with his lance near the Orewin Bridge. Then when he found out who he'd killed he cut off Llywelyn's head and it was put on show in English towns.

12 Some people believe the corpses are buried under the golf course at Builth Wells. But don't putter bet on it.

There's a stone at the nearby village of Cilmeri where Llewelyn fell.

It's a monument.

It says:

EIN LLIW OLOF

…OUR LAST RULER.

Llywelyn's body was buried at the monastery of Cwm-hir.

TWISTED TRAITORS

We're not sure if Llywelyn really was betrayed or if it was just an accident. Who might have betrayed him? One legend says he was betrayed by the Bishop of Bangor, another that Llywelyn was betrayed by the people of Builth. It's said the prince had been hiding in a cave to keep out of English hands. One morning he rode up to the blacksmith at Aberedw (near Builth) with a clever plan…

When the job was done Llywelyn rode off to Builth just before his English pursuers arrived.

Madog got the nickname Min Mawr... Big Mouth. And for years the poor people of Builth were called bradwyr Aberedw: Aberedw traitors.

TERRIBLE FOR TRAITORS

But there's another story that says the traitor wasn't Big Mouth Madog. It was much closer to Llywelyn's home. Maybe it was his own brother Dafydd that betrayed him.

He had a habit of betraying people so it's possible he sold his own brother to the English.

No one said that at the time – it's one of those legends that was told years later. We'll never know.

But if Dafydd DID betray his brother then he suffered an even more terrible fate than Llywelyn.

The story is too cruel to tell ... so I won't. But I will give you a clue. Here's the story with the nastiest bits cut out!

The missing words (in the wrong order) are:

guts   execution   eyes   English   body
stomach   horse   head   Welsh   neck

Dafydd was captured by the _____
He was handed over to the _____ who treated him as a traitor. And the punishment for traitors was brutal.
The sentence was read out. Dafydd, you will be taken from this place, dragged at the tail of a _____ to your place of _____ at Shrewsbury market cross.
There you will be hanged by the _____ until you are half dead. You will be cut down and woken up.
Then your _____ will be cut open and your _____ pulled out.
They will then be burned in front of your _____ as will your privy parts.
Your _____ will be cut off and your _____ cut into four parts for display above the walls of English cities.

Some reports even say his remains were attached to four horses and his body torn apart!

An old story says that when Dafydd was executed, he managed to take revenge on his executioner.

After Dafydd's body had been ripped apart by the horses, the executioner put his hand into Dafydd's mangled body and ripped out the heart[13].

He then threw it into a brazier of red-hot coals. Sadly (for the executioner) the still-beating heart jumped out of the brazier, with one of the coals attached. It hit him in the eye and blinded him.

The story was written about 120 years after the execution but it IS possible that a coal sparked into the executioner's eye and started the story of Dafydd's horrible heart.

Dafydd's head was sent to London and stuck alongside that of his brother Llywelyn! Cosy.

LLOVE THE LLANGUAGE?
....
Take Welsh llessons today!
Llearn for llife

13 The story says the heart was still beating!! That is REALLY unlikely. Ask your doctor or ask if you can tear a science teacher into four parts and see if their heart is still beating. Teachers like interesting experiments so they will say, 'Yes. Good idea.'

DID YOU KNOW...?

Perhaps the saddest victims were Llywelyn and Dafydd's children:

• Gwenllian, Llywelyn's baby daughter, was sent to a convent to be a nun and stayed there for the rest of her life until she died in 1337. She never knew her own true name.

• Dafydd's two sons were sent to live in a cage in Bristol Castle.

• One of them was still alive some 20 years later, by which time everyone had forgotten who he was and why he was caged.

HAVERFORDWEST HORROR

It wasn't just the English who were cruel in the Middle Ages. There were horrific crimes on both sides.

The governor of the castle at Haverfordwest captured a Welsh outlaw then tortured and blinded him.

The Welshman was allowed to live in the castle

and he made friends with the governor's son. The boy loved to hear the outlaw's tales of adventure. But the man kept his hatred to himself until one day he got close enough to the boy to snatch him.

He used the boy as a shield and made his way up to the battlements of the castle. He waited till the father came and begged him to spare the boy's life. But the Welshman threw the child to his death as the father watched. Then the outlaw flung himself after him.

IT'S A GREAT VIEW UP HERE

IS THAT SUPPOSED TO BE FUNNY

They do say the outlaw is suffering torture in the afterlife. One day he will return and haunt Haverfordwest Castle.

BIG ED

Llywelyn II was dead. Wales was without a prince and they hated the English King Edward I.

Big Ed started building beautiful castles to keep the Welsh in control. And he made the Welsh obey English laws. And in 1292 he charged them more tax than the English were paying!

No wonder they rebelled ... again.

In 1293 the Welsh rebels took the north-west of Wales – Gwynedd.

Edward defeated them at Maes Maidog. A few days later Edward's men massacred 500 Welsh soldiers while they slept.

PRINCE POPPYCOCK

Teachers for hundreds of years have told the story of how the first English Prince of Wales was crowned. Here is the teacher's side ... and here is how you might like to argue with it...

14 Yes some websites WILL tell you that lie! Don't believe everything you read on the internet.

111

NEVER MIND THAT NOW, GARETH. THE CHILD WHO GREW UP TO BE EDWARD II WAS THE FIRST ENGLISH PRINCE OF WALES

TRUE. BUT HE WAS GIVEN THIS TITLE IN LINCOLN, NOT CAERNARFON. CAERNARFON CASTLE WASN'T FINISHED TILL 1330. IN 1301 EDWARD WOULD HAVE BEEN STANDING ON A BUILDING SITE

AND THE WELSH WERE OVERJOYED. EVER SINCE THAT DATE THE FIRST-BORN SON OF THE ENGLISH MONARCH HAS BEEN MADE THE PRINCE OF WALES

THEY WEREN'T ACTUALLY – EVEN EDWARD II'S OWN SON WASN'T MADE PRINCE OF WALES

The Welsh were NOT overjoyed and many are still not happy with an English Prince of Wales.

In 1911 the Rhondda MP Keir Hardie said this:

There is to be a ceremony to remind us that an English king and his robber barons strove for ages to destroy the Welsh people. They succeeded in robbing them of their lands and driving them to the mountains like hunted beasts. The ceremony ought to make every Welshman blush with shame.

PUWER TO THE PRINCES 2:
ORFUL OWAINS

In the 1300s England went to war with France for 116 years[15]. Their star soldiers were the Welsh archers.

The French wars trained the Welsh warriors to fight…

AGAINST the English as soon as they had the chance.

And the chance came when a new leader, Owain Glyndwr (1349–1416), took them to war against the old enemy.

15 So of course the battles are known as the Hundred Years War … when really they should be called 'The Hundred years-and-a-bit war'. Wonder why they aren't?

AWESOME OWAIN

Owain Glyndwr was one of the richest of the Welsh landowners. BUT the revolt in 1400 wasn't about the posh people like Owain. It was a revolt of the peasants. Some of the Welsh peasants working in England even went home to take part. The Welsh peasants believed a prophecy…

> PROPHETS IN WALES HAVE SAID THAT THE WORLD IS COMING TO AN END IN THE YEAR 1400. PEASANTS WANT TO MAKE THE MOST OF THE TIME THEY HAVE LEFT. THEY HAVE ELECTED OWAIN GLYNDWR AS THEIR LEADER. WE MET SQUIRE GLYNDWR AT A PROTEST RALLY EARLIER TODAY AND THIS IS WHAT HE SAID…

THE EVENTIDE NEWS

> I PROMISE TO DELIVER MY FELLOW COUNTRYMEN FROM THE OPPPRESSION AND CAPTIVITY THEY HAVE SUFFERED SINCE THE DAYS OF CADWALADWR! I HAVE BEEN CHOSEN, BY GOD, TO RELEASE THE WELSH FROM THE SLAVERY OF OUR ENGLISH ENEMIES

The English tried to crush the revolt but storms smashed the English army. The rebels said God was on their side.

Many of the soldiers in the English army were Welsh. That could be very handy at times. In 1402 at Bryn-Glas the English Lord Mortimer saw a body of Welsh enemies on the hillside.

He ordered his English and Welsh soldiers to attack. It was madness. His English soldiers were slaughtered – but Mortimer's Welsh soldiers? They just said:

> HELLO LADS! NICE TO SEE YOU. WE WEREN'T REALLY FIGHTING FOR MORTIMER. WE JUST CAME ALONG SO WE COULD JOIN GLYNDWR'S ARMY!

Glyndwr ruled most of Wales by 1402 but hadn't captured any castles. He got help from the French … and from rebels in England!

ORFUL OWAIN

Owain Glyndwr could be pretty cruel in victory.

• It was said the castle keeper at Peterston-super-Ely was beheaded after he surrendered.
• When Owain Glyndwr took Radnor Castle, 60 prisoners surrendered. Owain ordered…

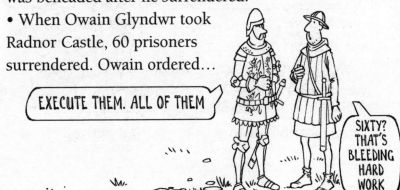

> EXECUTE THEM. ALL OF THEM

> SIXTY? THAT'S BLEEDING HARD WORK

• And Glyndwr's men wrecked the towns they defeated. Even 120 years later they still felt the effects. In Tudor times Sir John Wyn wrote…

I visited the towns of Hay and Radnor and they still bore the scars of Glyndwr's revolt. Green grass grew on the market-place in Llanrwst and the deer fed in the churchyard.

• Most horrible of all was Owain's battle at the River Lugg in 1402. A writer told what the Welsh WOMEN got up to.

That's horrible history.

OWAIN'S END

It was the future Henry V who defeated the Welsh. In 1405 he killed the Abbot of Llantarnam's army at a battle near Usk and the war turned against Owain Glyndwr. And, if you want a terrible tale, Owain's son, Tudor, was hacked to death and 300 Welsh soldiers were beheaded by the River Usk.

The war had turned against Owain.

• The French stopped helping him in 1406.

• By 1408 Owain's army had lost Aberystwyth Castle.

• In 1409 the English took Harlech Castle and captured Owain's family. But not Owain. No, he slipped away to the mountains to continue the fight.

And then...

• He disappeared! He may have died at his sister's house in 1415.

The rebellion failed and the Welsh were as badly off as ever. The squires of Wales tried to say Owain Glyndwr was just a crazy rebel – nothing to do with them.

But the poor never forgot him. Then in the 1700s Thomas Pennant collected the stories of Owain that made him out as the chief hero of the Welsh.

They say he's still alive. Sitting in a cave playing chess with King Arthur. Waiting for the day when the Welsh need a hero to save them!

> HOW WILL WE KNOW WHEN OUR COUNTRY'S HOUR OF NEED IS AT HAND AND IT IS TIME ONCE MORE TO JOIN IN BATTLE FOR THE RIGHTEOUS PROTECTION OF OUR GALLANT PEOPLE?
>
> WE'LL GET A TEXT

DID YOU KNOW...?

Owain was a pretty ruthless man. Even his own family suffered if they crossed him. Four hundred years after his death, an old oak tree was being shown to visitors...

> OWAIN GLYNDWR MET HIS COUSIN HYWEL NEAR HERE TO SORT OUT AN ARGUMENT THEY'D HAD
>
> SORTA KISS AND MAKE UP?
>
> THE COUSIN WAS A TRAITOR AND A FRIEND OF THE ENGLISH. WHEN THEY MET, COUSIN HYWEL TRIED TO KILL OWAIN BUT OWAIN WAS PREPARED. HE WAS WEARING ARMOUR UNDER HIS CLOTHES
>
> SMART MOVE

CAUGHT RED-HANDED

Owain of the Red Hand (Owain Lawgoch in Welsh, 1330–1378) planned to lead an invasion of England with the help of the French. In 1378 the English were so worried they found a way to stop him.

Owain of the Red Hand was at the siege of an English castle, Mortagne sur Gironde in Aquitaine, fighting for the French. Every day he used to sit outside the walls of the besieged castle and look at it.

He sat there every morning and combed his hair.

Now Owain had a Scottish servant. A man called John Lamb. Of course the Scots were at war with the English too.

One spring morning Owain was sitting on a log near the castle when he asked John Lamb to get his comb. (You had to comb your hair every day to keep the head lice under control.)

But when Lamb returned it wasn't just with a comb. It was with a spear.

He stabbed Owain to death. What for? For twenty pounds.

A history book at the time said he got away with it…

When he had done he left the dart in Owain of Wales's body and so went on his way into the English castle, for he knew the passwords to enter therein. Lamb told the leader of the English defenders that he had been under orders from the Duke of Lancaster to kill Owain, and so he was given shelter. Owain's body was carried by his companions-in-arms to the Chapel of St Léger, and was buried there.

SCRIBBLE
SCRIBBLE

Owain's army couldn't get their revenge on Lamb, so Lamb's friends were given the chop. Massacred. Lamb died peacefully in 1413 – 35 years later.

DID YOU KNOW...?

Owain of the Red Hand became a Welsh legend.
• It is said he sleeps below the ground on a throne.
• In his blood-covered hand there is a sword ... a sword that wins every battle it is used in.
• His underground tomb was once found by a young cowherd called Dafydd. But when Daf returned to rob the tomb of its gold he couldn't find the entrance. It has stayed hidden till this day.
• But some Welsh people believe that when the time is right Owain will awake and take over the throne of Britain!
So Queen Elizabeth II had better watch out!

TERRIBLE TUDORS

The 1500s should have been a good time for Wales. After all they had a Welsh family on the throne of England. The Tudors.

In 1485 Henry Tudor (1457–1509) landed at Milford Haven with a very small army. He hoped the Welsh would join him as he marched through the country.

MAKE ME KING AND I WILL MAKE WALES FREE AGAIN. I WILL FREE YOU ALL FROM YOUR MISERABLE SLAVERY

THAT'S NICE

He didn't keep his promises.

Henry Tudor's son, Henry VIII, took the throne, of course. He made Wales part of England.

In 1536 the 'Act of Union' brought the Welsh under English law.

At least they were EQUAL under the law.

LEE LAW

Henry VIII sent Bishop Henry Rowland Lee to be his top judge in Wales in the 1540s.

It was a shock for the villains of Wales. Before Lee came to Wales, most Welsh lords would keep murderers and robbers at their castles, look after them and share their loot. From now on the people of Wales would have justice.

But Lee was a racist. He said...

The Welsh are ALL thieves and villains. They are BORN thieves. So in my court a Welshman is guilty unless he can prove he is innocent.

What if the bully bishop was not sure that you had done the crime? He punished you anyway.

Bishop Lee spent a long time chasing Jones the cattle thief. At last Jones was caught and the bishop looked forward to seeing him swing by the neck.

Then came the awful news ... Jones had died in prison!

So the cattle thief's corpse was dragged into court. Lee gave the dead man a trial. He found the body guilty and sent it to hang.

They reckon Bishop Lee hanged 5,000 men in about ten years. Mothers used to tell their children...

YOU BEHAVE YOURSELF OR ROWLAND LEE WILL GET YOU

RED HANDED, RED BANDIT

There were lawless areas of Wales in the 1550s. Places where you wouldn't want to travel alone...

The Red Bandits of Mawddwy brought terror to mid-Wales for ten years, stealing sheep and cattle in the Dinas Mawddwy region. They attacked anyone travelling through the area. They are believed to have taken their name from their unusual copper-coloured hair.

Sir John Wynne of Gwydir rounded up their leaders and 80 of them were sentenced to death by the local sheriff Baron Lewis Owen. They used to meet in Mallwyd at the Brigands Inn and they were buried on Rhos Goch, the Red Moor, just two miles away.

One Red Bandit mother screamed at the judge…

> I CURSE YOU. ONE DAY MY CHILDREN'S HANDS WILL BE WASHED IN YOUR BLOOD!

Sure enough, on 11 October 1555 Owen was on his way to his home at Dolgellau when he was stopped at Dugoed Mawddwy. He was shot with 30 arrows.

DID YOU KNOW...?

While the Red Bandits were robbing in the centre of Wales the Red Bandit Robbers were working in the south.

They kidnapped a very rich English woman near Bridgend. They tied her manservant to a tree, then carried her off to the mountains till a ransom was paid.

HIGHWAY HERO

The Welsh seem to like their criminals – like the English love Robin Hood and the Scots admire Rob Roy.

The Welsh tell tales of a man from Tregaron called Twm Sion Cati.

He is better known to us as Tom Jones and was born in 1530, when Henry VIII was on the throne, and died in 1609.

Twm really did live near Tregaron but most of the stories told about him have been invented. Stories like the one about...

THE ROBBED ROBBER

Twm has been asked by the local squire to take a large sum of money from Tregaron to London. However, out in the wilds of West Wales, Twm is approached by a highwayman with a gun in his hand who says, 'Your money or your life.'

Twm throws his money to the ground but says to the highwayman, 'My master is a very harsh man, and he'll kill me for losing his money. Could you do me a favour and shoot two holes in my coat, so that I can show my master and tell him I put up a real fight?'

'All right,' says the robber, and he shoots a hole with each pistol into Twm's coat.

'Thanks so much,' says Twm. 'Now will you kindly shoot a hole in my hat, too?'

'Sorry,' says the highwayman. 'My pistols are both empty.'

'Well mine aren't,' says Twm. And he takes out his guns. 'Get down from that horse and give me your money.' Then Twm jumps on the highwayman's horse with all the money and gallops off to London.

DID YOU KNOW...?

Twm had a large farm near Tregaron.

There is a cave near Rhandirmwyn (between Tregaron and Llandovery) which is known as Twm Sion Catti's cave. He was supposed to have lived there.

Why anyone with a nice farm in Tregaron would want to live in a cave is a mystery!

TEST YOUR TEACHER...

This quiz is so easy even a teacher can get 3 out of 10! If you can't find a teacher to test then torment a traffic warden or niggle a neighbour.

1 In Roman times the Welsh invaded Rome and won. **True or False?**

2 In the Dark Ages English Bishop Garmon beat a Celtic army at Mold in North Wales by praying hard. **True or False?**

3 In the 850s the Welsh called their Viking raiders 'Black Devils' even though they weren't black. **True or False?**

4 In 1093 the Welsh besieged the Norman Earl of Shrewsbury's castle at Pembroke. The Normans were down to their last lump of ham. The Normans threw the ham to the Welsh outside. **True or False?**

5 A Welshman was the first man from Europe to discover America. **True or False?**

6 Welsh archers were the best in the world with their bows. But they were useless against knights in armour because the arrows just snapped. **True or False?**

7 An English monk said the Welsh were all thieves who would steal from enemies AND friends. **True or False?**

8 In 1469 at the Battle of Banbury, the Welsh were massacred because of an argument over a bed. **True or False?**

9 Enoch ap Evan had three heads. **True or False?**

10 In ancient Wales it was wicked to work on a Sunday. **True or False?**

Answers:

1 True … probably. There have been lots of great Welsh leaders – and the first was said to be Briton Maxim Wledig, known to the Romans as Magnus Maximus.

The story says Maxim saw the lovely Elen of Wales in a dream and in AD 368 travelled from Rome to Wales to marry her. Then he set off for Rome with her brothers in AD 383 to conquer the city.

He didn't do a very good job till Elen's crafty Welsh brothers worked out that the Romans went to lunch in the middle of the day. They built ladders and climbed into the city while the Romans were eating.

Maxim became Roman Emperor of the West until he was killed in battle against the Roman Emperor of the East. But at least for a few years the Welsh ruled the western world.

Some people say they still do.

2 False. He won by shouting at the Welsh! Garmon told his army, 'All we have to do is cry 'Hallelujah' and they will be defeated.'

Garmon's army screamed 'Hallelujah' and sure enough the enemy turned and ran away.

There's even a monument near Mold to show where this miracle happened.

3 True. They also called them…
- Black Heathen
- Black Host
- Black Nation
- Black Normans

And…
  Men from Dublin!

THEY'RE CALLING ME NAMES

4 True. The Welsh saw the ham and said, 'Shrewsbury's men are throwing food away. They can't be that hungry. They must have the castle stuffed with food. We'll be here years!' So the Welsh gave up and went home. Pembroke was saved.

5 False … probably. Most people agree the Viking Leif Ericsson discovered North America around AD 1000.

But in 1172 Madog ab Owain was fed up with all the fighting over his father's grave so he decided to set off to discover new land.

And who'd been in contact with the Vikings for hundreds of years? Who had fought against the Northmen and fought WITH them? The Welsh. If the Vikings could reach America so could the Welsh.

There are Cherokee Indian legends that say white men arrived from the East.

Welsh men?

And women. Because it is said Madoc returned to Wales, told the people of the wonderful new world and sailed back to settle there. They set up a tribe – the Mandan Indians in North Dakota.

6 False. Welsh archers were very skilled. A writer in the Middle Ages described one battle…

Another soldier had his leg, covered in armour, shot through by an arrow that pinned him to the saddle. He turned his horse round, and got a similar wound on the other leg, which meant he was fixed to both sides of his seat.

THE ARROWS ARE FALLING LIKE KNIGHT PINS

7 False. It was a Welsh writer who said that. Gerald of Wales was a monk writing around 1200 and he said:

> *It is the habit of the Welsh to steal anything they can lay their hands on and to live on plunder, theft and robbery, not only from foreigners and people hostile to them, but also from each other.*

8 True. William Herbert Earl of Pembroke (in Wales), and the Earl of Stafford (England) joined forces and captured Banbury town. The next day they had to fight the fearsome Earl of Warwick. But there was just one good inn room in Banbury. Pembroke took it – Stafford went off in a huff.

Pembroke's army had to fight without Stafford's help. They were smashed. William Earl of Pembroke and his brother Sir Richard Herbert were beheaded.

9 True. In 1663 Enoch (who had one head) was driven mad when his girlfriend dumped him. He saw his brother asleep with his head resting on the kitchen table. So he lopped off the head. Now Enoch had TWO heads!

When his mum came in and saw what he'd done he chopped her head off as well. So Enoch had THREE heads! He buried two but was arrested for murder and hanged.

10 True. There's a prehistoric stone circle at Moelfre Hill in Wales. The three stones are said to be three women who were turned to stone for doing a wicked thing … they worked on a Sunday!

And at Cottrell, South Wales, a stone circle is said to be women who gave false evidence that led to a man being hanged. How come no MEN get turned to stone in Wales?

MAD MODERN TIMELINE

The 1700s brought coal mines and steelworks to Wales. It also brought new religious ideas, not the squabbling Catholics and Protestants but the 'Methodists'.

— **1620** British ironmaking starts in Bersham in Clwyd (Flintshire) and the making of iron ore with coke.

— **1679** Catholic priests hanged and chopped at Cardiff Castle.

USE THE BEST! CHOP CATHOLICS WITH WELSH IRON

— **1735** Howel Harris is in church one day when he thinks Jesus has saved him. He starts telling other people and soon his new church – the 'Methodist' Church – becomes the biggest in Wales. Bad news – Methodists start up travelling schools for kids (to teach them the Bible).

BIGGEST IN WALES

NOT LIKE THAT

— **1761** John 'Iron-Mad' Wilkinson sets up factory at Bersham. He's mad about making iron … not mad about doing the ironing.

— **1792** The ancient meeting of Welsh poets – the Eisteddfod – is started again by Iolo Morganwg[16].

16 He used a ceremony he claimed to have discovered in an ancient Welsh manuscript. In fact Iolo wrote it himself.

1804 'Captain Dick's Puffer' starts running! It is the first steam railway locomotive, invented by Richard Trevithick and it runs in Wales.

1805 Welsh-American Oliver Evans invents the first steam-driven car.

1822 Now the Welsh are revolting. Miners form themselves into gangs called 'The Scotch Cattle'. Their aim is to stop strangers coming along and taking their jobs. Mainly the Irish who were starving in Ireland.

1831 Riots in Merthyr Tydfil. The army shoots 24 workers dead. But 16 soldiers are also wounded. The riot leaders are hanged or transported to Australia.

1839 Now the farm workers are revolting because they have to pay 'tolls' to use the main roads. Men disguise themselves as women and rob the toll gates. It's called the Rebecca Riots.

1841 A railway carries the coal from the Welsh valleys to docks at Cardiff. Welsh coal is sent off in ships. So Cardiff grows and grows into a big and brutal town. It is almost lawless.

1847 The English Church reports on why the Welsh make so much trouble. The report says: 'The Welsh are ignorant and lazy. The problem is that they speak Welsh and they go to their own Welsh churches.' The Welsh are furious.

1853 The valleys of South Wales are wrecked by the greed for coal. A visitor says the Rhondda Valley is: 'a picture of hell. The people are poor creatures boiling in sweat and dirt, amid their furnaces, pits, and rolling mills.'

1865 Some Welsh escape to the other end of the world – Patagonia in South America. They do well. There are still Welsh tea-houses there serving visitors today. It wasn't just the filth of the valleys that drove them away – it was death too...

1878 The Abercarn mining disaster – one of many Welsh coal disasters. Not all the bodies were found so many were left in the pit. One skeleton was uncovered some 27 years later complete with working clothes and boots.

1881 Welsh Rugby Union formed and South Wales has a new religion – rugby. But … the old Methodist religion gets Welsh Sunday Closing Act passed in 1881. No booze on a Sunday!

1900 A new century and Queen Victoria is dying. At Penrhyn Slate Quarry the miners go on strike but the owner, Lord Penrhyn, shuts the quarry for three years till their hunger forces them to return to work. New century, same old story for the poor Welsh.

PENRHYN'S MEN FEEL PENNED IN

CRUEL CRIME

The Welsh are not all thieves and villains, as Judge Lee said in the 1550s. But there have been some cruel crimes carried out in the country. Horribly cruel…

DUNRAVEN DOOM

In the times of the slimy Stuarts there is a tale too terrible to tell. So I won't tell you it.

The tale is about the Vaughan family and the castle they called Dunraven[17]. It is the tale of two men.

In the 1600s wicked Walter Vaughan lived in this castle by the sea[18]. Three of his children drowned in an accident in the Welsh waves, so Walter wrote to the king…

> Let me set up a lifeboat service. Pay me and I will save sailors from shipwrecks.

But the king said, 'No!'

Walter had just one son left and the boy sailed off to make his fortune. That's when Walter turned to the second man in the story that I can't tell you. His name was Matthew. This Welsh thief had been sentenced to have his thieving hand chopped off. Matthew had an iron hand fitted and became known as Matt of the Iron Hand.

17 It was really just a big house but 'castle' sounds posher so that's what the Vaughans called it.
18 Yes, I KNOW it's not a castle but I'll go on calling it that if you don't mind. Now shut up and let me get on with the story that is too terrible to tell.

Poor Matt must have had trouble wiping his nose.

Now Walter Vaughan had wasted his family fortune on wild living and found he needed cash. That's when he came up with a villainous plan. He called Matt of the Iron Hand to the castle one day and told him his plan to set up as wreckers…

So they began their wicked trade of wrecking. One of Matt's tricks was to tie lamps on to the tails of his sheep at night. As the sheep walked along the cliff top, the lights confused the ships and they crashed on to the rocks.

But Vaughan was in for a terrible shock.

It came one night when a fine ship was smashed on the rocks below Dunraven Castle … and a survivor swam ashore!

Matt of the Iron Hand was the first to reach him. The young man looked up at Matt and cried…

I simply can't tell you what happened next. You do not want to know that Matt chopped off the hand of the dead young man and carried it back to Dunraven Castle.

He threw it on Walter's desk to show him the fine ring he had saved from the sea.

And you certainly don't want to know that Walter Vaughan took one look at it and screamed…

It drove Walter Vaughan mad. He never recovered, they say. He took to drinking and wandering the beach where his son was murdered. He was raving. And when he'd done raving he went home to Dunraven.

Go there on a stormy night and they say you can still see the young man's cloak floating in the water.

IRON-HAND
HE'S JUST A MAN... WITH A-VENGEANCE
COMING SOON TO A THEATRE NEAR YOU

19 One legend says it was Walter, as the town magistrate, who ordered that Matt's hand be chopped off. Matt was just waiting for his revenge. But would Walter have been daft enough to trust him?

DID YOU KNOW....?

As for Dunraven Castle that wasn't a castle … it was knocked down in 1963. You can still visit the castle gardens at Southerndown though.

Just watch out for the Blue Lady who haunts them!

You know you've met her because she leaves behind a sweet perfume.

If she shows up then it's a sure sign there will be a disaster at sea. See?

WELSH WATER WARRIOR MAN

Some Welsh wonders, like Sir Henry Morgan, did quite well out of their crime careers…

1 Henry Morgan was born in Llanrhymny, Monmouthshire, and was from an ancient family going back to the Normans.

2 He was sent to the West Indies by Oliver Cromwell's government to attack our Spanish enemies out there. He was what they call a 'privateer'. That's a fancy name for a pirate!

3 But Henry wasn't a great sailor. He ran quite a few ships aground and wrecked them on reefs. Once he ended up clinging to a rock and had to be rescued. Very embarrassing!

4 Once, when he was commanding the *Oxford*, he went to his cabin for dinner. Some of the crew had had a drop too much rum and they went down to the stores to find some more. In fact the stores held gunpowder barrels, not rum barrels. The *Oxford* blew up beneath Morgan. 250 men were killed, but Morgan survived.

5 When he attacked Panama a lot of the men fell ill and the crew starved. Some of them had to eat their own boots.

6 The Spanish in Panama had a secret weapon. As Morgan's men lined up to attack the city they found themselves faced with the Spanish special defences.

The governor had a large herd of cows trained to charge Morgan's muskets. The cows got lost, turned around and charged the Spanish. But the governor still had time to set fire to the city and hide the treasure. Morgan won the battle but lost the loot. It was a glorious failure.

7 King Charles II knighted Morgan and sent him to Jamaica to build the capital city, Port Royal, and to govern the island.

8 Morgan drank himself to death.

LAMPETER LEGEND

Back in the 1600s a beautiful young woman called Ellen Lloyd lived in a house at Maesyfelin with her four brothers.

She was courted by a vicar's son from Llandovery called Samuel Prichard.

One day Ellen and Samuel were waiting in the Maesyfelin house. When the brothers arrived home Ellen and Samuel announced they were going to get married.

The brothers were furious. When their father died they'd have to share the wealth between the four brothers – but if Ellen married then they would have to share it with Samuel Prichard too.

They wanted to get rid of him. They tied him to the back of his horse and let it drag him all the way home to Llandovery.

It killed him of course. They cut the body from the back of the horse and threw it in the River Tywi.

His dad, the vicar, placed a curse on the Lloyd family AND on the house at Maesyfelin.

Believe it or not – it worked.

• First Ellen went mad with grief and died.
• Then the eldest son murdered his three brothers and hanged himself.
• And then the house burned to the ground.

This tale is probably untrue. It is just a story told by the folk of Lampeter to explain the ruin.

Ah, but less than a hundred years later that same Lloyd family had another terrible tale that almost certainly IS true. The stones from the ruined house were used to build a new house called Peterwell. But the curse went with the stones...

HERBERT HORROR

O ur story ends one evening in a gambling club in London.

It is August 1769 and the evil, grasping Herbert Lloyd of Peterwell sits with a gun in his hand...

I SAY LLOYD. WHAT ARE YOU DOING WITH THAT PISTOL?

DON'T WORRY MAJOR THE ONLY PERSON I'M PLANNING TO SHOOT IS MYSELF

YOU'RE DRUNK LLOYD, YOU LOST A LOT OF MONEY BUT IT'S NOT THE END OF THE WORLD. GIVE ME THE GUN

IT'S NOT THE MONEY, I'M TIRED OF THIS LIFE. DO YOU KNOW I COME FROM LAMPETER IN WALES? THE PRIEST THERE ACTUALLY PREACHED A SERMON AGAINST ME! THAT'S HOW EVIL I'VE BEEN. SIT DOWN, I'LL TELL YOU IF YOU LIKE

JUST EIGHT YEARS AGO I WAS A MEMBER OF PARLIAMENT FOR CARDIGAN BOROUGHS — KING GEORGE GAVE ME A KNIGHTHOOD. BUT THE PEASANTS HATED ME. THEY VOTED ME OUT LAST YEAR. IT BROKE ME. THEY HAD A GOOD REASON TO HATE ME YOU SEE. I OWN A HOUSE CALLED PETERWELL. FROM THE ROOF OF THAT HOUSE I COULD SEE NOTHING BUT MY OWN LAND. I BULLIED AND BRIBED EVERY LANDOWNER IN THE AREA TILL I GOT THAT LAND. THERE WAS JUST ONE MAN, ONE PIDDLING LITTLE FREEHOLDER CALLED SION WHO HELD THE LAST PIECE. I COULDN'T BUY HIM OUT SO I SPREAD A RUMOUR THAT SOMEONE HAD STOLEN MY BEST BLACK RAM. A HANGING OFFENCE IS THAT.

Herbert Lloyd's body was taken back to Peterwell and laid in the coffin ready for burial. But he owed people money. The lawyers had a notice pinned to the coffin. It said he couldn't be buried till everyone had been paid what he owed them.

There was a guard put on the coffin – and they stayed there for weeks to make sure he wasn't buried.

Remember, it was August. The body would go mouldy pretty quickly. Very mouldy – very smelly. In the end the servants at Peterwell got the guards drunk. They stole the coffin and buried it.

A terrible tale, but it brought an end to the family curse.

SILVER JOHN

John Lloyd was known as 'Silver John'. This is a short but sad little story that ended in the coroner's court around 1780.

I PROCEEDED TO THE BLACK BULL TAVERN AND GOT SOME OF THE REGULAR GENTLEMEN TO HELP ME CARRY THE BODY BACK TO THE TAVERN. BITS KEPT FALLING OFF AS WE TRIED TO CARRY HIM

WHAT BITS?

BIG BITS. HENRY PRITCHARD PICKED THE CORPSE UP BY THE ANKLES AND THE LEGS JUST SORT OF CAME AWAY IN HIS HANDS

I SEE. SO THE BODY WAS DECOMPOSED?

THE LAKE'S BEEN FROZEN FOR TWO MONTHS. I RECKON HE'S BEEN IN THERE THAT LONG. MOST OF THE LOCALS SAID IT WAS A BONE-SETTER CALLED JOHN LLOYD

WHAT DOES A BONE-SETTER DO?

HE SORT OF LAYS HIS HANDS ON ANIMALS AND PEOPLE WITH BROKEN LEGS AND HELPS THEM TO HEAL

SOUNDS LIKE MUMBO JUMBO TO ME. DO THE PEOPLE OF RADNORSHIRE BELIEVE THIS FAIRY-TALE STUFF?

THEY MUST DO, YOUR HONOUR, THEY PAID HIM WELL. HE ALWAYS HAD TO BE PAID IN SILVER AND HE STITCHED THE SILVER TO HIS COAT

AND WHERE IS THIS SILVER NOW?

And, most horrible of all, the Welsh people made up a little verse as an insult to the people of Radnor who let a harmless old man be robbed and killed. Children would sing it in the streets...

Silver John is dead and gone,
So they come home a-singing.
Radnor boys pulled out his eyes
And set the bells a-ringing.

DID YOU KNOW...?

Not all the crime in Wales was treason and robbery. There were lots of nasty 'little' crimes as well. In Cardiff there were street fights in 1598 with women as well as men joining in. One report said...

Today in Cardiff a woman's nose was split so it did hang down over her lips.

PAINFUL
PUNISHMENTS

Wales was the last place to 'press' a man to death. It sounds horrible. It is horrible.

It happened back in 1671 and the victim was Henry Jones.

• Henry wanted to get his hands on his mother's money and she didn't look like dying.
• Henry and a servant tricked the old woman into leaving the house. (Why? So there was no blood on the furniture, of course.)
• When they got her outside Henry shot his mother.
• The shot didn't kill her so the servant cut her throat with a knife.

• Henry Jones's sister helped cover up the crime. When it was discovered she was burned at the stake.
• The servant was hanged.

But Henry Jones was pressed to death. Why? Because he refused to plead guilty or not guilty.

At that time, if a man refused to plead then the court couldn't find him guilty – if they couldn't find him guilty then the court couldn't claim all his lovely money.

Jones took the pressing for two whole days then the jailers returned. He still refused to plead.

SIZZLING SAUNDERS

Mary Saunders was a serving girl in 1764. Just like Henry Jones she came from Monmouth. She loved fine clothes and would do anything to get some. Anything ... even murder!

She was the last Welsh person to be burned at the stake.

It would make a dramatic scene!

Smoking Saunders

Stage direction: The scene is a courtroom. A serving girl, in chains, stands facing the judge.

Judge: Mary Saunders. This court finds that in October 1763 you did murder your mistress, Joan Jones

Mary Saunders: I told you, I didn't do it. It wasn't me. I wasn't there and even if I was I didn't kill her. No way

Judge: Saunders, you took a meat axe and struck your mistress down

Saunders: Why would I do a thing like that?

Judge: Your motive was to steal her money. You have a love of fine clothes and ribbons. You murdered this harmless woman to satisfy your greed for satins and silks

Saunders: You're joking, aren't you? I wouldn't do a thing like that

Judge: The court has found you guilty. It is my duty to sentence you to death

Saunders: No! It's not fair. I only gave her a little tap on the head. I just wanted to send her to sleep while I nicked her stuff!

Judge: Usually the sentence for murder is hanging

Saunders: Oh, I wouldn't want that. Please don't hang me!

Judge: I'm not going to. Murdering your employer is treason. The sentence is to be taken from here and burned at the stake

Saunders: You what?

Judge: I could make it easy for you

Saunders: Easy?

Judge: I could tell the executioner to strangle you quickly before you are burned...

Saunders: Thanks, like

Judge: ...but your horrible crime deserves a horrible death. You will burn ... alive!

Saunders: (Screams) No! Hang me! Please hang me

Judge: Take her away to the stake!

Saunders: (Screams)

If you act out this scene do NOT send the actress up in smoke. Remember: Smoking kills.

CARDIFF COPS AND ROBBERS

Welsh iron and coal made fortunes for the iron-masters and the pit owners...

They had the job of selling it around the world. And that meant building great new docks. There were already docks in small ports like Llanelli, Pembrey and Port Talbot, but these were small, and Victorian ships were big. So great new docks were built in a little seaside town called Cardiff. It was pretty small until the docks were built. But the docks brought more than ships. They brought trouble.

Violence, street fighting and hooliganism. The locals thought mini-riots were quite normal and at first very little happened – they just stayed out of the dockland areas. A private police force was set up to sort out the worst of the trouble but they weren't very good. Reports say...

• Policemen were often drunk on duty.

• A Cardiff cop fell in the dock and had to be rescued.

• Two Cardiff cops jumped on a growling animal in the bushes ... but it turned out to be a drunken police friend snoring his head off – all three were sacked.

• Cardiff police managed to lose a corpse ... it was sent to the wrong place.

• A Cardiff policeman was fined for having a snowball fight with a customs officer.

And the brave boys in blue went in armed with swords. But it seemed to work. Still the police charge-book for Cardiff makes interesting reading today.

Which of these villains and crimes are **TRUE**? (**Clue** – TWO are made up ... but which two?)

№	Criminal	Crime
1	Bob the Goose	stealing a case of whisky
2	Jones the Jumper	stealing wooly jumpers
3	Oily Bob	stealing from a ship
4	Captain Cook	kidnapping
5	James Bond	stealing from the docks.

MERTHYR MURDER

The police DID manage to catch criminals. There were some cruel people in the tumbling towns that sprang up to dig coal and make iron.

Dick Tamar must have been one of the worst – violent and drunk, he killed his mum and stuffed her under the bed.

HORRIBLE HISTORIES NOTE

Don't try this at home. It ruins the carpet.

LOST
···
Corpse
If found please return to
Cardiff Police Station

Tamar was hanged outside Cardiff Jail in 1842 so Welsh people could see what happened to mum-murdering villains. A newspaper said…

On Friday afternoon the dreadful gallows frowned over the gateway to Cardiff Jail. Groups of people met to see the unhappy sight. Troops of beggars, cadgers, and speech-sellers arrived from all over Wales throughout Friday evening. During the night the lovers of the horrible came thick and fast into the town. The jokes were quite shocking. The executioner came to Cardiff early in the week. He was the famous Calcraft.

The 'speech-sellers' were people who printed out the last words of the hanged man and sold them – they usually made up the words!

Calcraft was so famous the gallows were known in the 1800s as 'Calcraft's toilet'. Nice.

TERRIBLE
TOURIST TALES

Wales is a popular place for people to go on holiday. But it hasn't always been so popular…

DREADFUL DEFOE

The writer Daniel Defoe (1660–1731) visited Wales in the 1690s and gave us an idea of what it was like in those days.

He didn't think much of it.

Mind you, the Welsh probably didn't think much of him. For a start his jokes were awful…

> *We entered South Wales. We began with Brecknock, a small inland county ... the English jokingly (but I think quite rightly) call it Break-neck. Haw! Haw! Haw!*

He was nasty about the towns.

> *Brecknockshire is mountainous to an extremity. The most to be said of this town of Brecon, is what indeed I have said of many places in Wales, that it is very ancient.*

Today's visitors love the mountain scenery. Defoe just saw the mountains as a nuisance.

> *Entering Glamorganshire we were greeted with Monuchdenny-Hill on our left, and the Black Mountain on the right, and all a ridge of horrid rocks and precipices between, over which, if we had not had trusty guides, we should never have found our way; and indeed, we began to regret our journey, as we did not meet with anything worth the trouble.*

In fact he wished he hadn't gone there!

This was a country looking so full of horror, that we thought we should have left Wales out of our tour.

Defoe was one of the first to see what Wales was going to be for the next 250 years – a land with mines and factories…

We came to Aberystwyth. This town is enriched by the coals and lead which is found in its neighbourhood, but is a very dirty, black, smoky place, like the people who looked as if they lived continually in the coal or lead mines.

He wasn't interested in the *Horrible Histories* tales of the past…

Then we came to Holy-well. The stories of this well of St Winifred are, that the good woman, was attacked and murdered, and a healing water sprang out of her body when buried… but this seems too much of a legend, to take up any of my time.

And he finished with a sneer at the Welsh people…

The Welsh people believe their country to be the pleasantest and most agreeable in the world, so you can keep a Welshman happy by letting him think you believe so too.

DID YOU KNOW...?

Anglesey has the village with the
longest place name
in Britain:

The name, in English, means...

The church of St Mary in a hollow of white hazel
near a rapid whirlpool and near St Tysilio's church
by the red cave.

But the name is a joke. It was made up in the
nineteenth century to attract tourists to the Island.
People of Anglesey just call it Llanfairpwll or
Llanfair PG.

GORY FOR GELERT

Unlike Defoe, most visitors like to hear old stories about a place. Horrible histories of what happened there in the past.

What if a Welsh village didn't have a terrible tale? Then the people could always make one up!

That's what happened with the tale of Gelert. In 1793 the owner of the Royal Goat Hotel came up with a great idea to attract visitors … the legend of how his village of Beddgelert got its name…

Beddgelert. It means the grave of Gelert.

So, who WAS this Gelert what is buried here?

It's an ancient and tragic story.

It all began with Prince Llewelyn the Great. He came to the valley once and camped there.

One morning the great warrior fed his baby son with goat's milk and left him in the tent while he went out hunting. Anyway, he left the child in the care of his great hunting dog, Gelert.

While he was away a wolf came into the tent and was just about to eat the baby. A tremendous fight took place … between the wolf and Gelert, not the baby and the wolf.

When Prince Llewelyn returned he found the tent in shreds and blood all over the hound. There was no sign of the baby. Llewelyn believed that Gelert had torn the child apart. Well, he would, wouldn't he?

He took his war spear and thrust it through the hound!

No sooner had the hound fallen to the ground than Llewelyn heard the baby cry under the torn tent. He pulled back the cover and there the child lay – without a mark on him – and the mangled corpse of the frightful wolf beside him. Llewelyn was torn ... only not as torn as the wolf, of course. Torn between joy at his son being safe and grief at the death of his dog. He turned to the dog ... the dying animal licked his hand and then expired.

Llewelyn mourned his dog like a lost brother and buried him with a hero's funeral in a marvellous tomb.

Stories like the one of Gelert the hound were harmless tales. Much worse things were happening in Wales in the 1700s – maybe. Take the strange story of a ruined house near Lampeter…

CRUEL CAP COCH

In 1790 revolution was raging in France. Many people wore red caps to show they were rebels. The French rebels killed the rich people and the Welsh redcaps were a peril to the posh.

And at the New Inn near Merthyr Mawr the innkeeper wore a red cap – he was known as Cap Coch … which is Red Cap in Welsh.

But Cap Coch wasn't a rebel, he was a murderer. If a lost and lonely traveller stopped at his inn he would rob and murder them.

JUST KILLING THE RICH LIKE OUR FRIENDS IN FRANCE

Was this just another horror story? A legend, like Gelert?

Cap Coch died. By 1840 the New Inn was in ruins and they knocked it to the ground.

Then, when they dug up the old cellars and in the fields outside, they found the skeletons.

Rather a lot of skeletons!

DID YOU KNOW....?

Turnspit dogs were in use until the middle of the
1800s to turn meat on a spit over the fire. The dog
was in a small wheel like a hamster – as the dog
walked forward the spit turned. It was hot and nasty
work so dogs were often kept in pairs – one day on,
one day off. That's why people say...

EVERY DOG HAS ITS DAY

Abergavenny Museum has the last example of a
turnspit dog, if you want to see him.

His name is 'Whiskey' and, of course, he is very
dead and very stuffed.

ROTTEN RELIGION

Wales has always been wild about religion. From the days of the dreadful Druids to the coming of the Christians, Wales has led the way to pray.

But not in the 1500s. As you know, Henry VIII brought the end of the monasteries. That was no big deal in Wales. The 13 Welsh monasteries only had 85 Cistercian monks in all.

But the monks looked after the poor and the sick – they suffered.

And the monks suffered – like one poor Welsh monk at Nevern in Pembrokeshire. His story was a truly terrible tale. The monk was put on a cart in a churchyard. A rope was thrown around his neck and the other end over the branch of a yew tree.

He spoke to the crowd…

The cart was driven away. Sure enough the sign appeared – a red stain ran down the side of the yew tree…

And they say that old tree at Nevern still bleeds to this day. Creepy or what?

MARYS AND MARTYRS

Mary Tudor came to the throne in 1553 and made everyone worship in the Catholic Church. Protestants were punished. Mary had the Bishop of St David's burned alive at Carmarthen.

Elizabeth I came to the throne and tried to turn Wales and England back to the Protestant religion.

The Welsh upper classes stuck to the Catholic religion pretty stubbornly.

Two Welsh squires joined the plot to set Catholic Mary Queen of Scots free and assassinate Elizabeth I in 1587.

Squire Thomas Salebury of Denbighshire in Wales and his chum Edward Jones of Plas Cadwgan suffered terribly in the Tower of London when the plot was uncovered.

PRIESTLY PAIN

Not all executed Welsh victims were guilty. Even as late as 1679 they were executing Catholics horribly in Britain. Take the terrible tale of John Lloyd and Philip Evans. It all began in England where a man called Titus Oates stirred up a lot of trouble.

Titus Oates was a fool. His nick-name was 'Filthy Mouth' because he swore a lot...

BUMS!

SNIFFLE

And because snot dribbled into his mouth.

He was an ugly creature with a low forehead, small nose, little piggy eyes, fat, wobbling chin, and a porky body. He also spoke with a squeaky voice

SQUEAKY BUMS

Then he met a man called Israel Tonge who hated Catholics. They came up with a scheme to make their name. They said there was a Catholic plot to kill the king. Catholics were arrested, tried and executed.

John Lloyd and Philip Evans from Wales were two Catholic priests living in Cardiff. They were arrested. The trial was a joke.

An old woman said...

I SAW THEM PREACHING A CATHOLIC SERVICE

But there was a reward offered by a man called John Arnold. So of course a poor woman would say anything for that sort of money.

DO I GET MY £50 THEN?

The judge told John Lloyd and Philip Evans to come back to his court in three months' time. He would tell them the punishment.

They could have run away, but they swore to wait till sentence was passed and they kept their word.

Philip Evans was brought the news of his sentence while he was playing tennis near St John's Church in Cardiff. When he heard the news he said:

WHAT HURRY IS THERE?
LET ME FINISH MY GAME

The sentence was horrific. The two priests were to be hanged, drawn and quartered at Cardiff Castle. Evans heard the news and sang and played the harp in his cell.

Evans stood on the scaffold, with the rope around his neck and said…

This is the best church any man can preach from.

Then they butchered him and John Lloyd horribly. Just for being priests.

Oates was shown to be a liar – but not until dozens of harmless Catholics had died.

He was dragged at the tail of a cart through London and whipped. They say he cried and bellowed like a bull.

RELIGIOUS REVOLUTION

In the 1750s, the Welsh were discovering a new sort of religion. There was a 'Methodist' revolution taking place.

It started in the 1730s with Howel Harris of Trefeca, Breconshire, as its leader.

CHILDREN SHOULD NOT PLAY, MEN SHOULD NOT WORK ON THE FARM AND WASHING SHOULD NOT BE HUNG OUT ON A SUNDAY

The Methodists brought Welsh Bibles into the homes and started Sunday Schools for both adults and children – they kept the Welsh language alive.

The Methodists said there was Hell in every one of us.

But even the Methodists had their terrible tales to tell. Howel Harris had his enemies. He went to Hay-on-Wye in 1750 and a mob killed his friend William Seward.

SIZZLING SUNDAY

The Methodists may have used the churches for preaching, but many other people used the churches for cockfighting.

Find·Out·How·Magazine

1. Hi, kids, today I'm going to show you how to enjoy the great old sport of cock fighting!

2. Great care is taken in the feeding of these birds. They have a diet of sweet butter with white sugar candy and rosemary, wheatmeal mixed with ale and whites of eggs

3. Here's how we train these two. First we put leather gloves on their spurs and let them fight without hurting each other

4. Cock fight day is a great day in a Welsh school. Every child in school has to give towards the Shrove Tuesday fights

5. We care for the birds before the proper fighting begins. The bird must be put into a basket, covered with hay and set near the fire. Then let him sweat. It makes him strong

6. If your bird is wounded then put your mouth against the wounds and suck out the blood. Then wash them with warm salt water.

F.O.H.M

7. Now we are ready for the contest. Sixteen birds fight in pairs, this is the Welsh way. The winners fight till they are down to four, then two, until we end with a winner

So the Methodists must have been happy about what happened at Pen y Bryn Chapel near Wrexham.

Go there and take a look behind the altar and you'll see a flat old stone.

It came from the local Berwig Quarry where cockfighting used to take place on Sundays in the 1800s.

One Sunday the cockerels were killing each other on this large stone. The money for bets was laid around the side. Then suddenly a flash of lightning came down…

It killed all the birds and injured most of the men.

The men were so shocked … electric-shocked … they took it as a sign from God. They gave up cockfighting and started coming to chapel instead.

They brought the stone with them as a reminder.

EVANS THE EXPLORER

John Evans was a Methodist from Waenfawr in Caernarfonshire. In 1792 he went to an Eisteddfod in Llanrwst and heard William Jones speak…

The Welsh people seemed to get behind the idea and backed an expedition. The bard Iolo Morganwg offered to go with young Evans.

The bard was 46 years old and decided to go into training for the expedition by sleeping out under the hedges.

Good idea? Not when the hedges are in Glamorgan. It brought on his lumbago (lower back pain) and it made him too ill to travel. Evans went off alone.

He reached America safely and set out on the thousand-mile journey.

He found the Mandans in the end.
He wrote one of the saddest letters ever.
'Ere, read it…

I have explored and mapped the Missouri River for 1,000 miles. I have spent a winter in the Mandan villages. However, the Mandans have no Welsh connections. I have to inform you that there are no such people as Welsh Indians.

The heartbreak killed young Evans. He went back to New Orleans and drank himself to death.

He was only 28 years old.

But … Mandan forts were built long before Christopher Columbus discovered America in 1492. It's said they were built like Dolwyddelan Castle. Even their language sounded like Welsh.

We'll never prove it now. In 1837 the Mandans were wiped out by smallpox.

But an American group, The Daughters of the Revolution, set up a sign which says:

> *In* memory of *Prince Madoc, a Welsh explorer, who landed on the shores of Mobile Bay in 1170 and left behind, with the Indians, the Welsh language.*

The Americans believe it!

BONFIRES FOR BODIES

A man called William Price brought cremation to Victorian Britain. His baby son died and Price burned the corpse on a hillside near Llantrisant. Price was taken to court and won the case – he said it was an ancient Celtic ritual. From then on cremation was legal.

When Price died in 1893 huge crowds turned out to see him cremated. They used two tons of coal.

MISERABLE MINES

In the 1700s, while the Methodist religion was sweeping through Wales, the 'industrial revolution' was getting under way.

Villages sprang up where they found coal or iron. Those villages turned into huge towns.

Mining town Merthyr Tydfil became the biggest town in Wales.

DEATH FOR DIC

The Welsh ironworkers wanted to protest against the dreadful conditions they had to live in. Tiny houses crammed together, disease and filth everywhere. Merthyr was crammed with 22,000 people. Twenty-five years before there had only been 7,000. No wonder the ironworkers wanted things to change.

In fact some died fighting for change. Men like Dic Penderyn...

The Cardiff Bugle

DIC DIES DECLARING 'I DIDN'T DO IT'

Saturday 13 August 1831 was the last day for Richard Lewis – commonly known as Dic Penderyn. He was hanged at St Mary Street, outside Cardiff Castle in front of a large crowd.

Dic was part of the Merthyr Riots back in May. The ironworkers of Merthyr went on a march for a better wage and to try and get the vote.

They marched into Merthyr and ransacked houses and robbed them.

One man in the crowd denied this. The man, known as Huw, said, 'We weren't robbers. The law officers had taken away our furniture because we were in debt. We were just taking it back!'

The ironworkers went on to raid the courtroom, steal the court records and burn them in the streets.

Huw went on, 'There was no need to send in the army. They shot twenty-four of the workers dead.'

But 16 soldiers were also wounded and that's what led to the trials. Twenty-eight men and women were put on trial.

They all ended up being sentenced to transportation to Australia. But for some reason Dic was sentenced to hang. Penderyn was found guilty of stabbing a soldier – but even the soldier said he couldn't identify Penderyn as the man who stabbed him!

It's said that the two men who accused Penderyn weren't even there. They were two hairdressers. But Dic had just had an argument with them. They hated him!

Still he died bravely. Dic Penderyn, hands tied behind his back, was led onto the scaffold by a minister.

Dic called 'O arglwydd, dyma ganwedd.' Our Welsh readers will know that means, 'I am going to suffer unjustly.'

The hangman placed a white bag over Penderyn's head and tied his feet. He pulled the lever and there was a gasp from the crowd.

As the man Huw said, 'Dic Penderyn – a Welsh martyr!'

Poor Dic was only 23 years old and he was probably innocent.

Forty years after the hanging, a man called Ieuan Parker confessed, on his deathbed, that he was the one who stabbed the soldier all those years ago.

Dic is remembered as a hero of the ironworkers. But in fact Dic was a miner!

CATTLE KILLERS

In the 1830s terror came to the miners in the valleys of South Wales. It was Edward Morgan and the 'Scotch Cattle'.

Here are ten foul facts:

1 Back in the 1820s the miners in the Monmouthshire Valleys decided to get together to bully the mine owners into giving them more money. In 1822 they went on strike and troops were sent in to control them. One or two miners were shot and the miners decided to fight back. These bullies formed themselves into gangs called 'The Scotch Cattle'. Their aim was to stop strangers coming along and taking their jobs. Poo!

2 Their victims were the Irish families who were starving in Ireland. The Irish would work for low wages and put the Welsh miners out of jobs. The Scotch Cattle gangs set out to drive the strangers away. They blackened their faces and each wore a head-dress with bull's horns on it.

3 Anyone who tried to stop them would suffer a raid on their home by a Scotch Cattle gang. They would smash open any door. If a mine owner tried to stop them then they would burn down his workshops. Phew!

4 They were crafty. Each valley had its own 'herd' of Scotch Cattle. They picked the biggest bully to be their leader. But they never attacked someone in their own valley – they always got another herd to do it for them. That way no one would recognize the wreckers.

5 They were secret societies – if you were a Moo and you betrayed your 'herd' then they would threaten to kill you. Yes, you!

6 They could come in and take everything except your food. They had a Scotch Cattle rule that they would never touch their victim's food. Then the kids wouldn't suffer.

7 But by 1834 the Scotch Cattle were getting out of control – beating up innocent people. One night they went into the house of Thomas Thomas in Bedwellty. There was a scuffle. A gun went off and Mrs Thomas fell to the floor. Dead. This time the Scotch Cattle had gone too far.

8 The leader of the gang was betrayed. His name was Edward Morgan. He was taken to court, of course. He was found guilty but he hadn't fired the gun that killed Mrs Thomas. He should have been sent to prison for life. True!

9 Instead, the judge decided Edward Morgan should hang at Monmouth Jail.

10 Morgan was hanged and the Scotch Cattle attacks died down after that. True.

CHEERLESS FOR CHARTISTS

In the 1820s the poor people of Britain decided they wanted the right to vote. They formed a group called the Chartists.

They were led by an Irish man and had a lot of support in Wales. They wanted to be peaceful – but of course it came to a messy end.

The Chartists had lots of enemies … enemies like Crawshay Bailey.

Crawshay and his rich friends were out to smash the Chartists any way they could.

On 4 November 1839 the Chartists marched down Stow Hill in Newport, South Wales.

The army was waiting for them in the Westgate Hotel. No one knows who fired the first shot but a battle took place and over 20 Chartists died. A newspaper report of the time made gruesome reading. The local paper, the *Monmouthshire Merlin* wrote…

Many who suffered in the fight crawled away, some showing frightful wounds and glaring eyes wildly crying for mercy and seeking shelter from the people; others desperately maimed were carried for medical aid, and a few of the miserable objects that were helplessly and mortally wounded continued to writhe in torture, showing in their gory agonies a dismal and impressive example of what happens to rebels and a sickening and sad spectacle for the eye of the loyal people.

Nine dead chartists were placed in the yard of the inn and made a deplorable sight. Many of the inhabitants of the town went to see them. A young woman forced her way through the crowd of spectators in the yard and no sooner saw the dead than she uttered a heart-rendering shriek and threw herself upon one of the bodies. The gush of fondness and of sorrow was great. She was dragged from the man she loved, the blood of the fallen rioter having smeared her face and arms.

A rainstorm soaked the rest of the marchers and spoiled their gunpowder. They just went home. But there were a couple more terrible tales to tell before it ended.

The leaders of the march were captured and were transported to Australia.

But MAYBE there were some traitors among the Chartist marchers. When they were discovered the Chartists MAY have executed them in secret.

There's a cave near Tredegar called the 'Chartist Cave'. Some people think the Chartists sheltered there after the storm. In 1970 it was dug open and the diggers found three skeletons from the mid-1800s – skeletons of men who had met violent deaths!

Had the Chartists executed the men who let them down?

IT'S A MYSTERY WITHOUT A KEY!

NOT EVEN A SKELETON KEY

HA HA

Britain banned slavery in 1807. But many Welsh workers were almost as badly off as slaves. They kept the workers so poor the children had to go to work from the age of seven. The Welsh worked for powerful iron-masters and coal owners. Rich and ruthless men – usually English.

CRUEL CRAWSHAY

One Iron-master at Nantyglo was the enemy of Crawshay Bailey – but his workers gave him the nickname 'Cosher'. Bailey had to build his family a little fortress in case the oppressed workers revolted.

Cosher Bailey decided he wanted one of these new steam train things and he would drive it himself on the Taff Vale Railway along the Aberdare Valley in 1846. He set off into a tunnel – and the tall chimney on his engine jammed against the roof.

The Welsh workers were so happy to see his disaster they wrote a funny song that they still sing today – 'Cosher Bailey's Engine'.

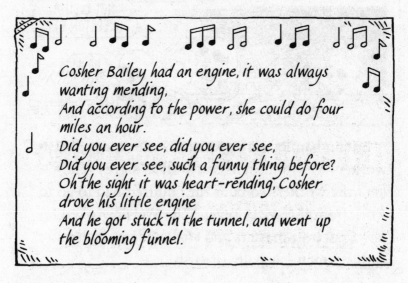

Cosher Bailey had an engine, it was always wanting mending,
And according to the power, she could do four miles an hour.
Did you ever see, did you ever see,
Did you ever see, such a funny thing before?
Oh the sight it was heart-rending, Cosher drove his little engine
And he got stuck in the tunnel, and went up the blooming funnel.

POETRY PROTEST

Another Welsh way to protest was to write a poem. This miners' poem was a simple story of a miner arriving at the golden gates of Heaven. He asks the door-keeper, St Peter, can he enter? Or will he be sent down to Hell?

Heaven or Hell?

A Welshman stood at the Golden Gate, his head bowed low,
He meekly asked the man of fate the way that he should go.
'What have you done,' St. Peter said, 'to gain admission here?'
'I merely mined for coal,' he said, 'for many a year.'
St Peter opened wide the gate and softly tolled the bell,
'Come and choose your harp,' he said, 'you've had your share
of Hell.'

SAD SWANSEA

The writer George Borrow travelled through Wales in 1854 and saw how the coal mines and steelworks had ruined the beauty of the valleys.

The Methodists had arrived in Wales and stopped people working on a Sunday. But 100 years later that was forgotten. Borrow said…

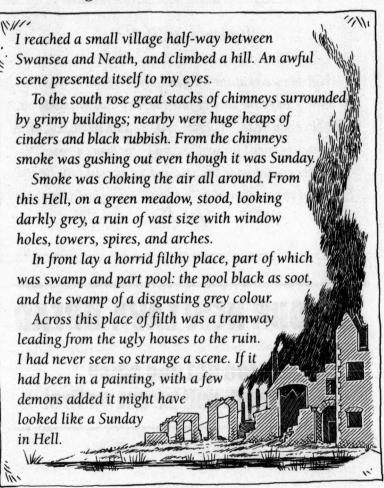

I reached a small village half-way between Swansea and Neath, and climbed a hill. An awful scene presented itself to my eyes.

To the south rose great stacks of chimneys surrounded by grimy buildings; nearby were huge heaps of cinders and black rubbish. From the chimneys smoke was gushing out even though it was Sunday.

Smoke was choking the air all around. From this Hell, on a green meadow, stood, looking darkly grey, a ruin of vast size with window holes, towers, spires, and arches.

In front lay a horrid filthy place, part of which was swamp and part pool: the pool black as soot, and the swamp of a disgusting grey colour.

Across this place of filth was a tramway leading from the ugly houses to the ruin. I had never seen so strange a scene. If it had been in a painting, with a few demons added it might have looked like a Sunday in Hell.

PEOPLE POWER

The Welsh have always been famously fierce fighters.

It's not just the archers in the Middle Ages who were savage scrappers.

MMA vs WWA

Can MIXED MARTIAL ARTS overpower the WELSH WARRIOR ARTISTES?

Find out, this Saturday

WILD WELSH WOMEN 3 – JEMIMA NICHOLAS

Everybody remembers the first French invasion of Britain in 1066 – they remember King Harold the hero who died with an arrow in his eye. But he was a man and a king so he's remembered even though he lost.

Sadly Jemima Nicholas (1750) and the Pembroke Mum's Army have been almost forgotten. She was a woman, of course, and it doesn't seem to matter that she actually won! (You might have been reading this in French if she hadn't!)

Here are ten famous facts about her dramatic – and almost forgotten – story.

1 On the 22 February 1797, 1,500 French troops, known as the Black Legion, landed at Carreg Wastad, near Fishguard, on the west coast of Wales. The main French army was planning to invade Ireland and set it free from British rule.

2 The French sent these 1,500 to attack Bristol – to make the English think THAT'S where the attack would be. But gales blew them past Bristol so they sailed round to Fishguard.

OU SOMMES NOUS?

BRISTOL FISHGUARD – WHO CARES?

3 The French expected the Welsh to rise up and fight with them against the English! Bad idea. But they picked a good place to land. The defenders only had eight cannon in the whole of Fishguard – and those cannon only had three cannonballs! So what did the defenders do? They fired blanks! It kept the French quiet for hours till Lord Cawdor arrived with a proper army.

4 The French found some barrels of wine that had been washed ashore the week before and they drank it all. There's a story that one Frenchman fell asleep in a farmhouse. He was so drunk he woke in the night and heard the click of a musket and fired at his enemy. It turned out to be the tick of a grandfather clock.

5 The local POSH people grabbed their money and ran away. But the peasants grabbed pitchforks and scythes and even spades and joined Lord Cawdor's army.

6 Jemima Nicholas – a local cobbler – went out into the fields that day and saw a dozen French soldiers wandering around. They were poor soldiers – half of the French army were criminals fresh out of jails. Some of them still had ankle irons on. They were starving and drunk. Jemima caught them chasing her sheep and chickens to eat.

7 She picked up a pitchfork and pointed it at them. They threw down their weapons. Jemima marched them down to the local lock-up. She became a Welsh heroine and was awarded a pension of £50 a year for life.

8 Jemima and her friends joined Lord Cawdor's army to attack the rest of the French on the beach – just to see the sport really. They caught one or two Frenchmen on the way. One was bashed over the head with a chair leg, another was thrown down a well.

9 The French on the beach saw the women's red cloaks in the distance. They thought they were more redcoat soldiers coming to attack. They threw down their weapons.

10 That's how a Welsh woman helped to stop the last invasion of Britain. But the French army was led by an old American, Colonel Tate. The last invasion of Britain was American-led. Not a lot of people know that.

After this defeat the French never tried invading Britain again. In fact no enemy has landed on Britain's shores since. (Unless you count a few German pilots shot down in the Second World War.)

REBECCA RIOTERS

The coal mines and the ironworks brought misery to many and made Welsh workers wild.

But life in the country was just as miserable as life in the towns.

No wonder there were Welsh troublemakers in the countryside as well as the towns.

In 1839 thousands marched on Carmarthen with a banner that said:

Their b-i-g problem was that the main roads had toll gates on them.

The Rebecca rioters started wrecking the toll gates in Carmarthenshire and Cardiganshire.

The riots spread.

HORRIBLE HISTORIES
TOP TIP FOR RIOTERS

In Glamorgan the rioters went to the toll-gate house and told the keeper…

20 There is a story that says the rioters borrowed the dresses from a woman called Rebecca … and that's where they got the name!

Boys. This is a great line when you next rebel against detention (dressed in the girls' uniforms of course).

Then they started to wreck the workhouses where starving families were forced to go, and they attacked the magistrates!

The police and army were called in. When they came to arrest Morgan Morgan his daughter attacked a law officer ... with a pot full of porridge.

The officers fired and wounded Morgan's son, John Morgan.

Morgan was transported to Australia and by 1844 the riots had faded out.

But those terrible tolls were cut – so the rioters won!

DID YOU KNOW...?

Morgan's son John recovered. And one of his ancestors went on to rule Wales! He is Rhodri Morgan, who became head of the Welsh Assembly in 2000.

EPILOGUE

Wales was a country of mountains and poor peasants. The Romans then the Saxons then the Normans kept trying to take over but they never quite made it.

English kings and queens called their oldest sons the 'Prince of Wales' but that hasn't fooled the Welsh.

In the end it was an English king Henry VIII who made Wales part of England. His laws crushed the Welsh language and made Wales just a little piece of West England. But Henry VIII was one of the Tudors… A Welsh family. How weird is that?

By 1800 there were half a million people in Wales. Then along came the coal mines and the ironworks. People rushed there for work. By 1900 there were two million people struggling to make a living in the filth and the danger.

The owners became rich but the Welsh people stayed as poor as ever.

The mines destroyed the beauty of the valleys and when the mines went the jobs went too. The ordinary Welsh were left poor … as usual. Of course the filthy pit heaps and the black clouds have gone too so the future is brighter … and so is the sky!

But Wales and its language was never crushed the way Henry VIII wanted.

By 1999 Wales had its own parliament again – the Welsh Assembly.

Maybe, like Owain Glyndwr, it will rise again. After all the horrible history maybe Wales will have a horribly happy ending!

INTERESTING INDEX

Where will you find the Black Death, putrid poetry and killer squirrels in an index? In a Horrible Histories book, of course!

TERRY DEARY

Terry Deary was born at a very early age, so long ago he can't remember. But his mother, who was there at the time, says he was born in Sunderland, north-east England, in 1946 – so it's not true that he writes all *Horrible Histories* from memory. At school he was a horrible child only interested in playing football and giving teachers a hard time. His history lessons were so boring and so badly taught, that he learned to loathe the subject. *Horrible Histories* is his revenge.

MARTIN BROWN

M artin Brown was born in Melbourne, on the proper side of the world. Ever since he can remember he's been drawing. His dad used to bring back huge sheets of paper from work and Martin would fill them with doodles and little figures. Then, quite suddenly, with food and water, he grew up, moved to the UK and found work doing what he's always wanted to do: drawing doodles and little figures.

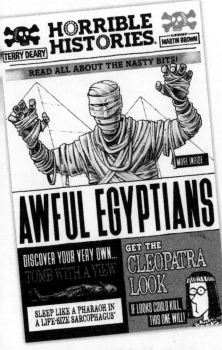

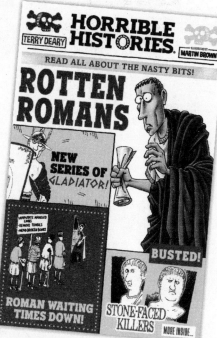

HORRIBLE HISTORIES.

TERRY DEARY · MARTIN BROWN

READ ALL ABOUT THE NASTY BITS!

CUT-THROAT CELTS

MORE INSIDE...

TURN YOUR *ENEMIES* INTO DRUID FLUID

WHAP

GET A **HEAD** WITH A NEW SWORD

TERRY DEARY · **HORRIBLE HISTORIES.** · MARTIN BROWN

READ ALL ABOUT THE NASTY BITS!

MORE INSIDE...

VICIOUS VIKINGS

THE GREAT VIKING RAID OFF
NEW SERIES · COMING SOON!

IF YOU MARRY MR. FLY-CUMMY
HAIR TODAY **GOWN** TOMORROW.

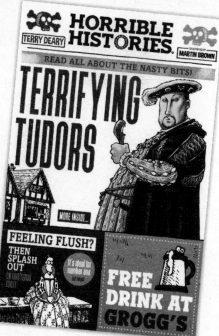